CONNECT FOR CLASSROOM SUCCESS

A Mentoring Guide for Teachers K-12

D1367287

CONNECT FOR CLASSROOM SUCCESS

A Mentoring Guide for Teachers K-12

R. Janet Walraven, M.Ed.

Copyright ©2019 by R. Janet Walraven

All rights reserved. No part of this book may be reproduced in any form or by any electronic or mechanical means, including information storage and retrieval systems, except with express written permission or where right to copy is designated within the text.

Every effort has been made to accurately present and credit quotations.

This book is not a work of fiction. Most names within chapter scenarios have been changed to protect the innocent, the guilty, and the author. The scenarios, stories, and mentoring advice are from authentic experiences. Dialogues presented resemble real situations as far as possible.

Author photo: Sarah H. Baker

ISBN: 9781096103189

Cover and Interior Design and Formatting by:

www.emtippettsbookdesigns.com

Dedicated to my parents, Sadina M. and W.E. "Bill" Walraven, for whom educating their three daughters was a paramount duty.

Thank you for your unconditional love, encouragement, high standards, and best-ever role modeling. You were lifelong learners.

PRAISE FOR THE AUTHOR AS TEACHER

Words cannot express the confidence you instilled in me. You held my hand, soothed my heart, and helped me to connect with my students. Your positive and kind message helped me grow as a teacher and as a person. Mentored Teacher

You changed my child's outlook on life. My daughter now loves school, can't wait to turn in completed quality assignments, and loves to read. Parent

After our mentoring sessions, I go back to my own world feeling so much better because you gave me your undivided, individual attention. First Year Teacher

I have so much respect for you as a teacher and a person. You are what I believe a teacher should be – tough but caring. Thanks to your mentoring and role-modeling, you've enhanced my teaching ability considerably. HS Faculty Member

Sharing, caring, and learning: You make life for those around you a wonder and a joy. Until your mentoring me, I didn't know teaching could be so gratifying. Junior High Teacher

You know how to experience life through the eyes of a child. Parent

You cultivated my love for knowledge. Thank you for teaching me to follow my dreams and to pursue living life with much vigor and joy. College Student

I learned so much from you; it was transformational. I loved the one-on-one attention you gave me. You helped me experience my own intelligence, helped me love myself, to think of myself as bright and capable and curious. You offered me the gift of imagination. I learned to participate in life because of you. HS Student

Modeling your zest for learning, creating, and caring changed the way I teach. HS Teacher

You treat students, parents, and colleagues with respect and consideration. Your energy and enthusiasm are contagious. Junior High Teacher

You are a passionate teacher who always puts her students first. You want the best for them and insist on quality work according to each's ability. School Librarian

Your dedication to our profession has been a constant source of inspiration. With dogged determination, you enhanced the lives of both students and teachers. Junior High Teacher

You are an articulate, bright, enthusiastic, gifted teacher. You brought new insights to our school; we continue to use your innovative ideas. Your contributions provided new life and energy to our department. HS English Department Chair

Lucky, lucky students who were blessed by knowing you. Thank you for your touch on our lives. Special Education Teacher

FOREWORD

I believe that all children can learn according to their own readiness, their own style, and at their own pace. I also believe that their depth of understanding varies. What I enjoy is teaching students to make maximum use of their minds; to understand how learning happens; to perform genius thinking with as much of their brain power as possible; to believe in their innate abilities; to believe in working smart to acquire additional abilities; to believe that though they may not have succeeded in past attempts, they can, with proper guidance, decide on a positive course of action.

I believe that *all children* have a genius of one kind or another. I like to waken that genius and help children learn to celebrate themselves. Reality says that by senior high some students choose not to turn that corner. I tend to think that I can win them all and am disappointed when I don't succeed. But I'd rather err on the side of optimism and risk disappointment than to overlook a student who might not appear to be success-oriented. *No child should be allowed to fall between the cracks.*

I hear some teachers talk about burnout in teaching. I do not believe in burnout. Many tasks in education can be draining, but it is not the kids who pull the plug. I prefer *to connect with each individual student.* Kids are energizers. I am happiest when I feel I am making a difference in their lives. Even the most challenging students stir my compassion for humanity and create in me a zeal to change the world one child at a time. I love the interaction with children as they learn. I love teaching.

One of the many challenges in teaching students who have been low achievers is that many of them cannot read well. If students are evaluated based on standardized testing, then educators must find a way to diagnose and prescribe for those students who have learning challenges. What I believe is that students often miss questions on tests, not because they do not have the knowledge or the ability *to think* adequately, but *because they cannot read correctly and efficiently*. Hence, they do not understand the questions. Also, many students who appear to be achievers, e.g., *gifted* students, are often merely good decoders of the written word but are not proficient in comprehension; they cannot read inferentially and excellently.

Education is truly the only hope we have for the future. If America is to progress as a free nation, we must teach children that freedom has a price, and that price is responsibility. Responsibility requires that we seek a deeper understanding of ourselves and all others. A truly educated mind continually seeks that balance between liberty and responsibility. A truly educated mind belongs to a lifelong learner.

This is my life's task: To waken in each student their natural passion for learning. It is the mandate of the American public to support educators in this endeavor. There is no higher calling than being a teacher. -R. Janet Walraven, M.Ed.

TABLE OF CONTENTS

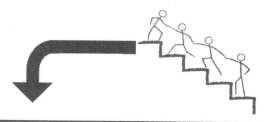

INTRODUCTION:

A TEACHER'S K-12 GUIDE TO CLASSROOM SUCCESS

Teaching is all about making connections with students, parents, colleagues, and administrators.

I taught K-12 for thirty-five years, mostly junior high and high school, in both private and public schools. Even though I have always been passionate about kids, learning, and education in general, my first seven years were rough. I struggled. I knew my curriculum. I knew how to teach subject matter. Here is what I didn't know:

- how to set up an efficient classroom
- how to organize reams of paperwork
- how to survive without working 18 hours a day and all weekend
- how to discipline students fairly
- how to connect with parents
- how to relate to administrators and colleagues
- how to get what I needed to succeed.

Statistically, a new teacher will spend five years or less in the classroom before giving it up. The majority of those teachers could become stellar teachers if they had the proper support.

I took workshops on everything I could find that would help me with those struggles. I learned from every source possible. Those first seven years were enough to make me want to quit. What I needed was an experienced, successful mentor…or a guidebook like this one. As I struggled through the first few years, I became disenchanted with trying to fit into the "normal" way of teaching. That prompted me to start my own K-8 accredited school– a project that turned out to be extremely challenging, financially and academically, but one of the most gratifying experiences of my life. I was, in effect, my own mentor. As an administrator and teacher, I consciously focused on learning from every challenging situation. During the next few years, after putting certain strategies in place, I finally felt like I was getting a handle on the situation. I'm grateful now that I stayed the course.

I wrote this book to show you how to connect the pieces and complete the puzzle. Whether you have been teaching for three years or twenty-three years, my hope is that these scenarios will help you meet even the most difficult challenges. No matter how long you have been teaching, you and your students deserve to enjoy each day in your classroom with excitement, gratification, and even **joy.**

CONNECT FOR CLASSROOM SUCCESS is all about helping you become a successful teacher.

No human being will work hard at anything
unless they believe they are working for competence.
William Glasser

Teaching is not for the faint of heart. Without intrinsic motivation, it can be the most frustrating and difficult profession in the world. With authentic motivation, it can be the most creative and gratifying.

Can you relate to any of the following?

- A student refuses to engage in the learning process.
- An irate parent reams you out over the phone, or worse, in person.
- An administrator calls you on the carpet after someone complains.
- A peer questions or criticizes your methods.
- You are exhausted and wonder why you ever chose this profession.
- Students complain that you lost their papers, that you graded them unfairly, or that your teaching is not relevant to their lives.
- You observe bullying but don't feel supported in reporting it.
- You know you are expected to contact parents but can't find the time, and in all honesty, put it off because you feel intimidated.
- You feel overwhelmed with living in a paper factory.
- You want to be one of those popular teachers but can't seem to make it work.
- You want to feel in control of your classroom.
- You feel nickeled-and-dimed buying things for your classroom.
- You dread facing parents at back-to-school night or conferences.
- Sunday nights bring a sick feeling in the pit of your stomach.
- You create a great lesson plan but don't have time to grade it.
- You resent spending your entire holiday grading papers.

- You find a note passed in class depicting you as a witch.
- You feel like some of the students know more than you do.
- You get your paycheck and know you could be making more money with less effort in the corporate world–or even as a waiter with good tips.

If you reacted to any of the above, this book is for you. I offer tools to make your teaching life easier, more efficient and productive, more gratifying, and best of all—more pleasurable.

Are you willing to make your first professional priority that of genuinely connecting with your students, their parents, your peers, the administration, and your community? If so let's get started....

———————◆———————

Effective teaching may be the hardest job there is.
William Glasser

CONNECT WITH STUDENTS:

FEEL AT HOME IN THE CLASSROOM

Providing a safe environment is generally left up to the administration with teacher and staff support. What I'm talking about here is actually *feeling at home in the classroom*—a feeling of belonging. A sense of place is paramount for all students.

On the first day of school, and after that when a new student enters the room, take time to orient the students to what is there for them and where the boundaries are. The following is the setup for a junior or senior high English class. Customize it to fit your needs.

Start with tissue issues, and believe me, it can be an issue for a lot of teachers and students.

SCENARIO:

Ms. J: *Good morning. Let me introduce you to Puffs.* [Hold up a box of tissues—not the cheap one-ply grocery store brand—the soft, strong, 3-ply Puffs.] *These Puffs are yours. You may help yourself whenever you need one. You don't have to raise your hand to ask; just get up out of your desk and get one or two as needed. Just so you know, I buy these with my own money, and they aren't the cheap kind, so please use only what's needed, but feel free to use what's needed. [Smile!] These are soft and comfy and won't be abrasive to your delicate noses. Do you know why Puffs? Because you are worth it. Now moving on....*

[Jose grumbles.] *What was that, Jose?*

Jose: *I was just saying that last year the teacher had a roll of toilet paper in the front of the room, and it was embarrassing to use it. Thanks!*

Ms. J: *You're quite welcome. I don't like using toilet paper to blow my nose either.*

Right next to the Puffs is the sanitary hand gel. Please use it after blowing your nose or whenever you feel you need to cleanse your hands. I'll not go into my lengthy explanation of how many germs we all bring to the classroom. Just use your head about it, and let's all help each other stay healthy.

Next to that is a spray cleaner and paper towels. Use it whenever you feel your desk needs to be cleaned. I use it once a week on all the desks and doorknobs, the buttons on the boom box, the pencil sharpener, and anywhere else all our grubby hands have been. Feel free to use it whenever, but keep the spray confined to a small area.

Next, we have a ceramic coffee mug filled with pens and pencils. If you forget yours, feel free to take one of these. They aren't new, but they are usable. If you have extra, feel free to contribute to the cup. Next to the cup is the electric pencil sharpener. Use it any time you need except when anyone is addressing the class. [Invest in an electric sharpener. Students grinding away on a mechanical sharpener is unnecessary noise, makes a mess, and listening to it is a daily stress. Find one that has a nice soft hum.]

The plants at the windows are there to enjoy. They usually flower during the winter. Won't that be nice? [Smile!] Once in a while, they get a bit dry. Here's the watering can. If you notice they need water, please go get some, and we'll all share in the beauty. Just a caution: Better to underwater than overwater.

Next comes the boom box. It's really true what research says about learning better when listening to Mozart. Some of you might take a week or so to get used to that, but you'll find you like it. If I forget to turn it on, please take it upon yourselves to do so or remind me. There are several CDs here to choose from. We'll adjust the volume to match whatever we are doing in class at the time.

And what is this? This is the mystery box. Does anyone still like to get a prize inside their cereal box? Once a week I'll put a mystery question on the inside lid of the box. If you feel like playing the game, read the question, put your answer in the box, and Friday is prize day. Once in a while, the prize will be extra credit points. Not required; just for fun. [See **Odds and Ends** for *Mystery Box*.]

Here in this bookcase, you'll see reference books—dictionaries, various types of thesaurus, spelling aids, writing aids, etc. Feel free to look through these or use them whenever you want. Yes, you may use them during tests, even for spelling. By the way, what makes a good speller? Someone who knows how to spell almost anything, or someone who knows when to look up the correct spelling of a word? [Rhetorical question. Pause to hear the sighs of relief.]

Notice the recycle bin. It's just an ugly old box. I'd love for one or two of you to decorate this appropriately for us. Let me know if you're interested. Please recycle used paper. Once a week I'll be happy to entertain volunteers to take this down to the main recycle container. Some schools have an organization that comes around to pick up recycled paper. That's nice. Maybe some of you might like to get that started through your student organization.

On this back wall is the birthday calendar. If you want your birthday recognized, please add it to the calendar. If your birthday comes when school is not in session, make up an alternate birthday. You'll be treated to all of us singing "Happy Birthday to You." My birthday is also on the calendar, and I'll be most happy to have you sing to me! If you want to bring treats on birthdays, all the better!

Right beside the birthday calendar is a mirror. Feel free to check for spinach in your teeth, clean up that bloody nose, comb your hair, or just see how wonderful you look.

Moving along, here we have a lovely army-surplus file cabinet. The bottom two drawers are out of bounds for all of you. There's nothing sacred in them—no *test papers or confidential materials—just stuff you don't need to be into. The top two drawers are organized with information dealing with topics we'll be discussing—photos of writers, some interesting things I've picked up in my travels that we can use to create Shakespeare scavenger hunts, a bunch of Okie/Route 66 items, and other treasures. Just find the tab that relates to what we're studying or, whenever you feel like it, let me know if you want to do an extra credit project. You may find interesting items to contribute. Once in a while, remind me to dig through the drawers for surprises.*

Let's talk Potty Breaks. No, we won't be using a paddle or shoe or any of those disgusting insanitary bathroom pass objects. I'm going to provide, in your planners, two bathroom passes for each of you at the beginning of each quarter. You each have time between classes to go to the bathroom—well, most of the time.

NOTE: Most schools provide planners for students, or they purchase their own. Instruct the students to turn to the calendar for the first day of the quarter and write *Pass One, Pass Two.*

When you need a pass, bring it to me without interrupting or saying anything. I'll initial it, and you're on your way. But hurry back! At the end of the quarter, I'll give 5 extra credit points for each bathroom pass not used. No, these are not transferable. If any of you have a medical situation, bring me a doctor's note, and I'll be glad to honor that confidentially. By the way, guess what happens if you lose your planner.

This takes no time, no discussion, and eliminates those students who habitually try to get out of class. This may or may not apply to lower grades. [See **Odds and Ends** for *Bathroom Passes K-5* and *Passes 6-12.*] You may also want to have a short discussion regarding emergencies.

And last, here's my desk. [Stand protectively in front of your desk. Narrow your eyes, raise one eyebrow, and look into the eyes of each student.] *This is the only sacred area in the classroom. Do not sit at my desk, do not touch anything on my desk, do not sneeze on me or my desk, do not ask to borrow my pens or pencils, and do not touch my computer. Did everybody get that?* [Nod your head yes until they are all doing the same.] *Good.*

Now I'm going to ask you all to fill out a questionnaire about yourselves, just so I can get to know you a bit better. While we're doing this, please take turns writing your birthdays on the calendar. Here are some fun colored pens to use in case you want to decorate your day.

NOTE: By this time, the students have generally relaxed, maybe laughed a little, and someone has tested you by getting a Puff, looked through the top drawers of the file cabinet, or used the hand sanitizer. The first brave person to venture from their desk has given others permission to do the same. Let them wander around a bit. Encourage them to feel it is their space and that it's good to feel at home in a classroom. Remember this: It's your space, too, and you deserve to have it as comfortable as possible.

———— ◆ ————

One looks back with appreciation to the brilliant teachers, but with gratitude to those who touched our human feelings. The curriculum is so much necessary raw material, but warmth is the vital element for the soul of the child.

Carl Jung

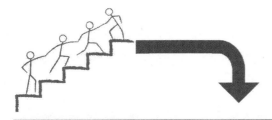

CONNECT VIA THE WORM GAME:
NAMES MATTER

Names are important. They are the icing on the cake of our identity. As a student in your classroom, I want to know that I am important and special enough for you to want to know my name from the first day.

If you teach in elementary school, you probably have thirty names or less to learn. If you are in middle, junior, or senior high, you will have upwards of 100 names to learn.

The Worm Game works, no matter whether it's kindergarten or high school. Remember, too, that when you get new students at various times during the year, they also have to start from scratch getting to know everyone. Play the Worm Game each time a new student enters your classroom. You might even try it in a teacher workshop where few know each other by name, hence, role-modeling for their own classrooms.

THE WORM GAME

All stand or sit in a circle—make it an even circle—perfectly round—so each person feels included and can be seen equally by all. No slumping or ducking behind someone else. Being seated on the floor is easier for younger children.

Focus on first names only. A game may be played later to learn last names.

Hold up a pencil and say: *This is Worm, and I am* _____. (Fill in the blank with your name.)

Hand Worm to the person on the left. S(he) says: *This is Worm, that is (pointing to the person on the right)* _____, *and I am*_____ *(Fills in own name).*

Hand Worm to person on your left; repeat all the way around the circle. Each person introduces Worm and has to repeat each previous person's name in order. You, the teacher, are last and must repeat all names. If you have a new student in class, place that new student last so they learn all the names, including yours.

NOTE: Keep students on task, looking and listening to each other respectfully. Explain to them that our names are an important part of our identity, and we need to respect that.

If a student gets stuck remembering, only the one being identified may give his or her name. Let those two interact. No coaching from other students. You will notice that this may be the only time some of the quieter students get to hear their peers say their names. Require students to speak up and enunciate.

If a student has a shortened name, e.g., Barb for Barbara, ask the student which they prefer. If they say, "It doesn't matter," respond with, "Yes, it most certainly does. You choose. It's your name." Most students have a preference.

———— ◆ ————

A name pronounced is the recognition of the individual to whom it belongs.
He who can pronounce my name aright, is entitled to my love and service.
Henry David Thoreau

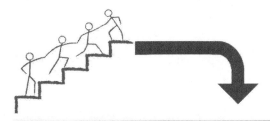

CONNECT THROUGH DIALOGUE:
MANAGE RATHER THAN CONTROL

I wish teachers who want to preach would become just that—preachers. Note the difference. Engage the students in dialogue so that they can discover for themselves the importance of the lesson. Each student deserves a classroom environment conducive to learning efficiently. Your task is to maximize that opportunity. Convey to them that they have a responsibility for their own learning as well as a responsibility to enhance the learning environment for their classmates.

Never ever humiliate a student.

SCENARIO 1: First day of school. 9th grade classroom. Establish parameters. Be explicit. Students need to know exactly what the boundaries are. Modify for any grade level.

Ms. J: *I have only one rule in this classroom:* ***Be courteous.*** *Can anyone give me an example that is not covered by that rule?*

Sam: *Can we chew gum?*

Ms. J points to the sign. **Be courteous**: *Does the rule fit, Sam?*

Sam: *Okay, if I chew gum with my mouth closed and don't throw my trash on the floor and don't put my gum under the desk, then is chewing gum allowed?*

Ms. J: *The answer is yes. You answered your own question, Sam. Thanks for clarifying that.*

[Julie raises her hand.] *Yes, Julie.*

Julie: *I was going to say, if someone is passing a note to another student, but it didn't disrupt anyone else, would that be discourteous?*

Ms. J: *What do you think?*

Scott [speaking out without raising his hand]: *It's not courteous if you're not paying attention.*

Julie [using a *neener-neener* tone]: *And you're not courteous because you didn't raise your hand.*

Scott: *Do we have to raise our hand every time?*

Ms. J: *What do you think works best?*

Scott: *It's hard to have a good discussion if you have to wait to say something every time.*

Julie: *What if two students speak up at the same time?*

Scott: *You didn't raise your hand.* [Julie blushes.]

Ms. J: *What about it? Let's get back to the original guideline.* **Be courteous.** *Does that cover your question?*

Scott: *I guess if I want to speak up at the same time as someone else, I could let them go first. That would be courteous.*

Julie [addressing the teacher]: *So, do you have a rule that says we have to raise our hand and wait to be called on?*

Ms. J: *I have only one rule:* **Be courteous.** *I'll let you answer your own question. 'Nuf said. Thanks for the clarifying discussion.* Leave it there and let them think about it. The next time something comes up, reiterate the rule or point to the poster/banner/sign that you have on the wall that says: **Be courteous.**

NOTE: Teachers sometimes overstate the obvious. You've given them the *Be Courteous* rule and walked through a couple of examples via dialogue. All you need to do from now on is point to the sign, or as needed, ask someone in the class to state the rule. Let the students own the rule; expect them to correct their own behavior and use positive reinforcement to help their peers. When a student is totally out of line, verbally or otherwise, a stern but smiling reminder from you—*I'm at this moment giving you an opportunity to correct your behavior*—is sufficient.

Remember: **Do not humiliate any student.** If a more serious situation occurs, ask the student to step out into the hallway for a private conversation. Next step: Make a parent/guardian phone call. See *Discipline Procedures* at the end of this chapter.

In more serious situations, know your building procedures for calling the office or security for backup. Use this only when absolutely necessary. Don't be guilty of crying "Wolf." The office catches onto that quickly, and you may find yourself ignored.

Everyone needs a claim to fame. A student who cannot get attention, or positively establish an identity, will choose a negative path. This may be overt or covert. Your job as teacher is to connect with each student in a way that directs them onto a positive path toward success. Think of yourself *as managing rather than controlling the classroom environment.*

SCENARIO 2: Ninth grader Joel's goal seems to be to establish himself as the class clown. His antics are overt—pulling a girl's hair, dropping his book loudly on the floor during the teacher's presentation, asking to go to the bathroom, breaking a pencil and tossing it across the room.

The teacher ignores the antics and merely points to the **Be courteous** sign. Joel continues acting out. Some students shoot him a dirty look; someone says quietly, "Knock it off." The teacher-pet-wannabe says, "You know the rule:

Be courteous." Joel retorts with a mimicking snarl, "Be courteous," and grabs her paper. As soon as the class is busily working on the given assignment, the teacher taps Joel on the shoulder. "Please step out into the hallway. We need to talk." Joel follows with mock arrogance, looking around to see if the other kids are watching.

Ms. J: *Joel, you've been very busy this morning doing your best to disrupt the class. I have to give the other students credit for doing an excellent job ignoring you or giving you some good advice. I need to know why you feel these antics are necessary.*

[Joel drops his head, stands on one foot, doesn't look you in the eye.]

Joel: *I'm sorry, Teach. I'll do better.*

Ms. J: *Please be respectful enough to look at me when I'm speaking to you.* [He looks up sheepishly.] *Sorry doesn't cut it, Joel. Just "sorry" doesn't mean anything. Actions speak louder than words. I'll give you this one warning. Any further antics and we call a parent conference. Is that clear?*

Joel: *Got it!*

NEXT STEP: Don't lie in wait for Joel to mess up. Let him know you are there to help him succeed. Go out of your way to give him positive attention. Disallow his claim to negative fame. Kids are generally very tuned in to a teacher's method of operation. He'll get the picture quickly. We all want affirmation and approval. If kids aren't getting it at home, yes, it is your responsibility to fill the gap. Wear the hat proudly!

Express yourself in terms of *need* rather than *want*. Students want a lot of things they don't get, and they don't care what you want. What we all *need* is much more important than what we all *want*. Example: Rather than say, I want you to sit down and be quiet, say, *Please sit down. Please be quiet. We all need your cooperation.* Here's another one: [Parents take note!] *How many times have I told you….* What you're really asking is for the class smart-aleck to start counting, *Well, let's see, Teach, I'd guess around 100 times….* If you've told them once and given them a courteous but strong reminder, that's enough.

Don't repeat yourself. If need be, single out the culprit and remind about consequences.

> **NOTE:** Follow up by finding out what Joel's skills are. First and most important question in any kind of disciplinary situation: Can the student read efficiently and correctly on grade level or above? See Chapter on **Read Right.**

SCENARIO 3: Seventh Grade. Star athlete Jake asks if he can go talk to the coach.

Ms. J: *Not now, Jake. You have an assignment to work on. Stop in on your own time and make an appointment with him.*

Jake: *But I really need to go see him about the game this afternoon.*

Ms. J: *I answered your question. Please sit down and get to work.*

Jake: *But...*

Ms. J holds up her hand for a *stop signal*, points to the **Be Courteous** sign, and motions for him to sit down.

End of discussion. Jake grumpily goes to his seat and, after a few minutes of stubbornness, resumes working on his assignment. Stop by his desk and quietly say, "You made a good decision. I appreciate your cooperation."

> **NOTE:** See chapter on **Recognition as the Greatest Motivator.**

Recap of Discipline Procedures

- ◘ Establish parameters.
- ◘ Engage the class in dialogue, giving them an opportunity to own courtesy.
- ◘ Disruption #1: Give the student an opportunity to correct behavior. Check student records. Make yourself aware of the student's skill level. If it's lower than grade level, take responsibility for getting whatever help the student needs. Follow through with the student.

- Disruption #2: Have a private conversation with the student. Regardless of skill level, the student can learn to behave within the parameters of the classroom.

- Disruption #3: Call parent/guardian and set up a conference if necessary.

- Further disruption: Ask the administration for a staffing that includes student, parent/guardian, counselor, and administrator. Expect the group to find a solution. Follow through with a plan. If necessary, ask the student and parent to sign a contract for committing to succeeding. Numerous examples of contracts are available online. Choose one that fits the situation or make up your own. [See **Odds and Ends** for *Success Contract.*]

NOTE: At about six months of age, most children earn an *MM degree—Master Manipulator.* Your job as teacher is to sabotage that intent. If you are used to having a chain that students yank by "making you mad," get rid of that chain. Do not allow students to manipulate your emotions. Discipline is a fairly simple matter of setting parameters and following procedures. The challenge is to do that consistently. [See **Odds and Ends** for *Courtesy Contract.*]

———— • ◆ • ————

You do not control your classroom environment;
rather, you learn to manage it effectively.
Personal Creed of R. Janet Walraven

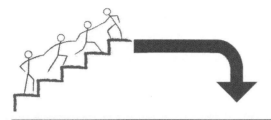

CONNECT WITH PARENTS:

A STITCH IN TIME...

Before the end of the third week of school, contact each parent/guardian at least once. Yes, even in secondary when you have over 100 students. You will find the time spent exponentially worthwhile. If at all possible, make the first contact positive. [See **Odds and Ends** for *Parent/Guardian Contact Log.*]

The temptation, and perhaps the need, will be to start with parents of students who immediately alert you to disciplinary procedures, i.e., the challenging students. As far as possible, continue through the list alphabetically or devise your own method. I like to mix it up so I have a nice balance of positive and negative phone calls. If possible, leave a message and follow up. Do not leave it up to the parent to return your call. Tag pages of "No answer; left message; call back." Continue through the list as rapidly as possible. No excuses; it's your responsibility. You need to do this. Life will be astoundingly easier later on if you do.

Enjoy those calls to parents/guardians telling them, *Hi, I just called to tell you what a pleasure it is to have Susan in class. She is extremely attentive and turns in work on time. Thank you for your good parenting.* Be prepared for a long pause or a stuttered response. Your call will be such a surprise that it will usually last only a minute at most. You can fly through the list of the easy kids. Enjoy!

The following day you will be met with stunned students who want you to know that they know you called home. Good or bad, you have made an important connection. The impact is huge on both parents and students and usually leads to immediately improved behavior. You may also learn valuable information that will come in handy later.

Whether the contact is in person or by phone, be sure to make notes on the *Contact Log.* Get parent/guardian permission to call them at work when necessary. Make notes as to how supportive they seem. If a situation arises in the future, you should be able to refer to your notes for an idea of how to handle the issue. Make the notes work for you.

NOTE: Administrators appreciate teachers who take the time to contact parents. Earn a reputation for doing so. If a negative situation arises later, you will have earned the backing of your school team. Be willing to show your contact log to your administrator if the situation calls for it.

SCENARIO 1: Teacher calls a parent to compliment the student.

Ms. J: *Hello, this is Ms. J, Shawna's English teacher.*

Ms. Miller: *Hello, I'm Shawna's mother. Is there a problem?*

Ms. J: *No, not at all. In fact, I called to tell you what a delight Shawna is. She is so attentive in class, turns her assignments in on time, and does beautiful work. I always look forward to reading her papers. She's quite a good writer.*

Ms. Miller: *Oh, my. I've never had a phone call like this before. Thank you. Thank you so much. You've made my day. I'll let Shawna know. In fact, I'll take her to lunch this weekend. I've wanted an excuse to do just that. Thank you again.*

Mrs. J: *My pleasure. Have a good evening.*

NOTE: Take time to make the positive calls. Parents of children who sit quietly doing their work day after day do not often hear praise from teachers. In fact, I would venture to guess that the easy kids rarely, if ever, get a call home.

SCENARIO 2: Teacher calls home to speak with the guardian/grandmother of an 8th grader.

Ms. J: *Hello, Mrs. Johnson. This is Ms. J. Your granddaughter is in my Language Arts class. I'm calling to find out if Kaitlyn has a good place to study at home. She hasn't been turning in her work on time.*

Grandmother: *Well, I'm sorry about that. I do all I can, but I just can't make her sit down to do it. She won't listen to me. Ever since her mom took off after my son was put in jail, I've done all I can. You people at the school expect me to work miracles. Getting her to do her homework is your job.*

Ms. J: *Thank you for that information, Mrs. Johnson. I'll see what I can do to help Kaitlyn at school. Is it okay if she stays after school some days? Shall I give you a call if I keep her after to help her with her work?*

At this point, the grandmother will realize you are not critical of her and that you really want to help Kaitlyn, or she will just blow you off. Either way, take a deep breath, be courteous, and stay in a positive mode. You're doing the best that you can, too, and whether or not she wants to acknowledge it, she'll know that.

NOTE: Never allow yourself to become defensive with parents or students. Keep the emotion out of the situation.

SCENARIO 3: Teacher calls home to advise the parent that the student has vandalized a computer keyboard.

Ms. J: *Hello, Mr. Heckle. This is Ms. J. Jeremy is in my computer class, and I'm sorry to let you know that he hasn't been responsibly handling the equipment. Do you have any suggestions, or is there something you can do to impress upon him how using expensive equipment is a privilege?*

Mr. Heckle: *My son is not the problem here. You obviously don't have control of your classroom. If you were the watchdog you're supposed to be, there wouldn't be a problem.*

Ms. J: [First, remember to breathe. He put you on the defensive. You are merely stating facts; no emotion involved.] *I'm sorry you feel that way, Mr. Heckle. Jeremy dismantled the keyboard and is responsible for the cost of that. I need to remind you that you and he signed a contract for the use of computer equipment.*

Mr. Heckle: *That may be, but I'm not responsible for his behavior in your classroom. I will not pay a dime for any equipment.*

Ms. J: *Thank you for your time, Mr. Heckle. I'm sure I can work this out with the administration. Have a good evening.*

NOTE: Turn this situation over to the administration. Log the call with details. You've done all you can at this point.

SCENARIO 4: Parent comes barreling into your classroom after school.

Parent: *I want to know why you're allowing my son Joey to play basketball when he's not passing your class. You know the rules!*

Ms. J: *I can see you're upset. Would you like to sit down so we can see how to resolve this?* [Take a seat even if he doesn't. This puts him in a power position, and that's what you want him to feel.]

Parent: *No, I don't have time. You fix this. I've laid down the law to my son about getting his work done. He needs to get good grades so he can get a scholarship and get into a good college. I had to take time off work to come down here. What are you going to do about it?*

Ms. J: *I'm sorry you had to take time off work, but I do appreciate your caring. I have talked with the coach about this situation. But as you know, your son is one of the best players on the team. The coach has bent the rules to benefit the team. It's out of my hands.*

Parent, softening when he sees you are on his side: *I'm sorry. I didn't mean to come on so strong. I'm just so frustrated about this.* [At this point, he'll probably sit down.]

Ms. J: *I understand. Would you like me to set up a meeting with the coach and Jeremy's teachers so we can all be on the same page with this? I'd be happy to arrange that. When would it be convenient for you?*

NOTE: By not allowing yourself to become defensive, you have turned the parent's anger into compliance and solution. Follow through with making arrangements convenient for the parent. Be sure to prepare the other staff members and administration with the necessary information so they don't get blindsided. Ask for and expect administrative support for following school guidelines.

SCENARIO 5: Second week of school. Geometry class. Ms. J has just explained the basic concept of lines and planes.

Kevin [interrupting Ms. J]: *I just don't get what all this is about. There aren't lines shooting off into space, and there aren't these invisible planes going in all directions out in the universe. This stuff just doesn't exist, so why do we have to study it? Let's do some real math.*

Ms. J: *Excuse me, Kevin. I appreciate your skepticism, but what I'm asking you to do is open your mind. You like music, right?*

Kevin: *Yeh, but don't try to con me. Music has nothing to do with this. You can't win me over; I'm onto you.*

Ms. J: *What I want you to understand, Kevin, is that music and math are universal truths that go together. They are yin and yang. Give this a chance; I think it will all come clear.*

Kevin: *No way....*

Ms. J: *Kevin, before you say anything else, I want you to decide how to approach this class and me with respect. I've indulged you a bit much, and now it's time to give the other students a chance to learn.*

Kevin: *You can't shut me up. My dad will be down your neck.*

Ms. J: *I look forward to talking with your dad, Kevin. Does anyone else have a question or comment?*

The students sit silently. Kevin, red-faced, fumes quietly.

Later that evening....

Ms. J: *Hello. May I please speak to Mr. or Mrs. Langston?*

Parent: *This is Larry Langston.*

Ms. J: *This is Ms. J, Kevin's geometry teacher. Do you have a few minutes?*

Mr. Langston: *Yes, of course. Let me guess—Kevin smart-mouthed in class.*

Ms. J: *Well, let's just say he's not afraid to ask questions in a rather challenging way. What I need is for him to learn to ask those questions with a bit more respect for me as well as respect for the rights of other students to have equal time in class. Do you think you could talk to him about that?*

Mr. Langston: *I'd be happy to, and I'm glad you called. I appreciate that so we can get off on the right foot. Thanks for taking the time.*

Ms. J: *You're welcome. I'll look forward to seeing Kevin in class tomorrow. Please feel free to drop in or call me if you have any questions. I believe students do much better when parents and teachers communicate regularly.*

Mr. Langston: *That's a breath of fresh air. You can count on it. Kevin's mother and I want to be involved as much as possible. Let us know if we can be of help at any time.*

Next day. Kevin enters the room early. Ms. J is at the board writing the daily assignments.

Kevin: *Good morning, Nice Teach-er.*

Ms. J. smiling, turns to face him: *Good morning, Nice Stu-dent.*

Looking a bit sheepish, Kevin returns the smile. The connection is made and lasts throughout the year and beyond.

NOTE: The incident in the classroom was not allowed to escalate. A few minutes spent contacting the parents resolved the issue of respect. Kevin never did learn to like geometry, but he did his lessons without complaining and often assisted other students who were struggling. What made the difference? Soliciting parent support early in the year.

SCENARIO 6: Jeremy is a polite student but often falls asleep in class.

Ms. J: *Hello, this is Ms. J, Jeremy's English teacher. May I please speak to a parent or guardian?*

Grandmother: Yes, this is Jeremy's grandmother.

Ms. J: *Are you his legal guardian?*

Grandmother: Yes, I am. Is Jeremy in trouble?

Ms. J: *No, nothing like that. I'm just a bit concerned. Jeremy is behind in his homework and seems to be struggling to stay awake in class. I just wondered if there is more I can do to help him. I've asked him to stay after school for additional help, but he said he has to work.*

Grandmother: Oh, I'm so sorry. Jeremy helps me with my cleaning business, and I'm afraid he stays up a bit late during the week. I clean offices, and it has to be done at night. I wish I knew another way, but since his parents were both killed in an accident last year, and my husband passed away just a couple of months ago, it's all I can do to make ends meet. I just don't know what else to do right now.

Ms. J: *It's Mrs. O'Leary, right? Would you mind if I talk to the school social worker and have her contact you? Maybe the three of us can come up with some way to help Jeremy. He's so very polite, and I can tell he'd like to do well in school. Would you mind if we work on a solution together?*

Mrs. O'Leary, tears in her voice: Oh, my, I can't thank you enough. I just didn't know where to turn. Jeremy is such a sweet boy. I'd appreciate any help you can give him. I'll look forward to hearing from the social worker.

Ms. J: *I'll have Ms. Silvey call you this week. Thanks for taking the time to talk with me. In the meantime, I'll shorten Jeremy's assignments until we can work something out. Have a nice evening; I'll be in touch.*

NOTE: Be careful not to judge a student's lack of progress before finding out all of the details. Most students truly want to succeed. Make the phone call and search for resources to help solve the situation. Talk with the school counselor, the school social worker, or your administrator. Help is usually available in most situations.

Connection is the energy that exists between people
when they feel seen, heard, and valued.
Brene' Brown

SCENARIO 7: Teacher calls the parent of a senior who may not graduate.

Ms. J: *Hello, this is Ms. J. May I speak to Doug's mom or dad?*

Mr. Hearst: *Yes, this is Doug's dad.*

Ms. J: *Mr. Hearst, I just wanted to let you know that Doug's grades are slipping a bit, and I'd like to enlist your help so we can work together to help him succeed this year.*

Mr. Hearst: *First of all, I'm a single dad. I leave early and come home late. I try, but, well, Doug is a latchkey kid, as they say. I've talked to him about the importance of school. Since he's a senior this year, he's old enough to make his own decisions. He has a job, a car, and a girlfriend. I'm afraid he is prioritizing in that order. As much as I appreciate your phone call, I'm leaving this up to him. I'll tell him you called, and I'll try to encourage him, but I'll leave the rest to you. Don't get me wrong. I love my son. But he needs to make choices and reap the rewards or suffer the consequences. Thanks for your time.* [Click]

NOTE: Okay, you can't win them all, but you need to give it your all. Now it's up to you to do what you can to help the student learn to prioritize. The important thing is that you made the call to the parent. Now work to make a connection with the student at school.

The most powerful way to connect to another person is to listen.
Just listen. Silence often has far more power to heal and to
connect than the most well-intentioned words.

Rachel Naomi Remen

———— ◆ ————

Teaching is a record of failure, but the glory of teaching is in the attempt.

Pat Conroy

CONNECT WITH THE CHALLENGED LEARNER:

DISCOVER THE REAL PROBLEM

I would prefer that we didn't label children at all, and that the first label we do away with is *slow* or *challenged learner.* We often use labels because students are not meeting the stated objectives or the expectations set for them. We fail to recognize their talents as well as fail to recognize the specific areas that have *slowed them down.* Our first question should be: *What is the real problem?* As educators, we often get the cart before the horse. The cart is everything else there is to learn. Reading is the horse. Students need proper neurological makeup to read excellently. I know how, using the **Read Right®** methodology, to make that happen. You can learn it, too, if you're willing. It's a true paradigm shift from the way we have always believed reading should be taught. Teaching it takes a willingness to change, and that's exciting.

EXAMPLE 1: Julie exemplified all the traits of a *slow learner.* By 8th grade she had become withdrawn; she wouldn't hold her head up to look an adult in the eye, and she chose to be with a negative peer group. Even though her grades were above average through 4th grade and she was a very social child, her parents said they didn't know where their little girl went. *Solution:* Once Julie was identified as a non-reader, that problem was taken care of with time spent in the **Read Right** program. She gradually returned to being a bubbly, self-confident young lady, succeeding in school and looking forward to leadership responsibilities.

EXAMPLE 2: Jimmy was a very gregarious 7th grader. He loved learning and was way beyond his peers in knowledge, vocabulary, insight, and experience. However, Jimmy could not read beyond the 2nd grade level, so he was labeled a *slow learner*. Gradually, as he began being shunned by his peer group, he became a loner. *Solution:* He was put into a special reading class, i.e., **Read Right**, where he was brought up to grade level within one year. Jimmy's self-esteem rose rapidly. He decided pursuing knowledge was his favorite past-time, and within two years earned an award as a stellar student.

EXAMPLE 3: Donald was three years old when a traveling optometrist found him begging in the streets of Columbia. The good doctor adopted the child and enrolled him in American schools. Educators determined that Donald was *slow* and told the doctor that Donald would never learn to read. *Solution:* A dedicated teacher made it her goal to change that perception with the help of the **Read Right** program. Beginning the program in 9th grade, Donald learned to read at grade level by the end of 10th grade. Through his reading, he learned how to set goals and soon caught up to his level in other subjects.

EXAMPLE 4: Meredith, a senior, was a straight-A student but always needed more time to finish tests. On track for becoming valedictorian, she was in a panic. Hearing about the **Read Right** program from her classmates, she approached the teacher.

Meredith: *It's two weeks until graduation, and I'm panicking about college. I stay up half the night getting my assignments done, and if there's a timed test, I seldom finish it. Would you test my reading and see if you can help me?*

During the oral test, the **Read Right®** teacher was shocked to hear Meredith read with extreme stuttering that was not at all noticeable when she spoke. Meredith admitted to knowing that the stuttering also occurred while reading silently. Though the **RR** teacher had no experience with this phenomenon, she agreed to **RR** sessions before, during lunch, and after school. Due to Meredith's maturity and commitment, she completed the program in only two weeks. The stuttering was gone. She became an excellent reader.

NOTE: The number one problem for challenged learners: *They do not read correctly.* Solve the problem by using reading techniques that *correct the problem rather than compensate for the problem.* **See ReadRight.com.** Along with this correction is the need for teachers, administrators, parents, and the community to work in partnership to give these students "an extra scoop" (Google *Continual School Improvement* or *CSI*) of understanding, compassion, specific strategies for more efficient learning, and the ability to embrace the idea of succeeding. We must focus on individual solutions rather than the label of the *slow or challenged learner.*

All children and adults can learn to read at the same level at which they speak. Please—I am begging you—take time to go to *ReadRight.com* and see how you can miraculously impact the lives of your students. It will be the most rewarding teaching you have ever experienced.

NOTE: Read Right is available to train staff in schools, prisons & detention centers, corporations, and community-based organizations. RR offers online tutoring via video conferencing software for children, teens, and adults. They also offer RR as Second Language tutoring.

————◆————

Lives hang in the balance.
If you do nothing else as a teacher, develop able and passionate readers.
Rafe Esquith

CONNECT THROUGH EXCELLENCE IN READING:
THE READ RIGHT® METHOD

My personal passion is a program called **Read Right** [www.readright. com]—a research-based program that provides an environment that compels the brain to learn to read excellently. I've referred to **Read Right** in several other chapters. I cannot stress enough the importance of this topic to the success of all students.

QUESTION: Why is American education slipping so far behind, and what can we do about it? One possible solution is **Read Right**. I personally think it's the only real solution.

Eighty percent of children do not read excellently; yes, I said 80%. Now, before you object, I did not say they don't read; I said they don't read *excellently*. I've had 10th grade honors students who *sounded fluent* but seriously lacked in comprehension.

Did you know that everyone can learn to read as well as they know how to speak? It's true. I have used **Read Right** with children grades 2-12, children who were labeled with everything from ADHD to severely mentally-challenged. I even taught a 65-year old educator who had his master's degree (and his administrative degree!) how to read excellently. Yes, he knew the basics, but reading was slow and uncomfortable. His love of history motivated him to press on. After retiring from education, his goal was to write a history book. To gather the information he needed, he read—a lot, but the process was laborious. He just could not get through the books efficiently.

One day he tentatively approached me with the request, "Do you think you could help me read better?" My response: *Absolutely!*

Because he already had a wealth of experience, knowledge, and excellent vocabulary, within a couple of months he was zipping through the books, enjoying every minute, and wondering why on earth he hadn't learned to do that before. Now he's writing books!

What is the silver bullet? A program called **Read Right**, developed by wonder woman Dee Tadlock, Ph.D. (She'll chafe at my calling her that.) By the way, the label *silver bullet* is my own, and I sincerely believe the program is just that. If every school in America used **Read Right**, our education system would be #1 in the world of education.

What I have never figured out is how anyone expects students to learn without being excellent readers. When are we going to harness that horse to the front of the cart instead of dragging him behind? I repeat this metaphor because it is apt.

How did I stumble upon **Read Right**, and why don't more people know about it?

I can answer the first question; you'll have to ask Dee Tadlock for the answer to the second question.

As a teacher in K-12, most often in junior high and high school language arts classes, I was smart enough to know what I didn't know. For sixteen years I struggled to help the majority of students with schoolwork that they were not doing well. When a student is failing, acts out, or retreats, you can bet it's because they are not an excellent reader. Everything I tried turned out to be nothing more than compensating techniques. I went to every workshop I could find on how to teach reading, but I instinctively knew that those techniques were not getting to the crux of the matter. I knew what I needed was some way to understand *how the brain learns to read.*

Needing a solution to this dilemma, I turned to my advisor at the University of Washington where I previously completed a Master's in Education. In a conference with Dr. Tim Standal, he recommended that I pursue a program linking neurology with linguistics. That sounded daunting but exciting; I was ready to do whatever it took to reach my goal.

Synchronistically, my school district sent me to a technology workshop. What piqued my interest was a presentation on- guess what – *How the Brain Learns to Read.*

Dee Tadlock, a nice-looking, professional, personable woman, sat at a round table with eight or ten other interested teachers. As she explained how the brain learns to read, I could hardly contain my excitement. This is exactly what I had been looking for and what I wanted to learn to do. Dr. Tadlock had already discovered the answer.

After convincing my school district to adopt the **Read Right®** program, I became a certified **Read Right** tutor. Using the program was like watching daily miracles. The extreme was a 9th grade non-reader who was told he would never learn to read. By the end of the third year with **Read Right,** he was reading at grade level. Another student, a seventeen-year-old severely developmentally disabled student who seemingly could not read beyond the 1st grade level, progressed to reading at 4th grade level within two years. *He could read as well as he could speak.* The valedictorian of the high school who had hidden her reading disability, eliminated her problem in just a few weeks—a great relief to her as she entered college.

These are extremes. The average gain is one year of reading ability for every 15 to 18 hours of instruction time *with no regression.* If a student in 8th grade reads on a 3rd grade level, that student can catch up to grade level in one year. Check out the website for the statistics, philosophy, research, and results. Every time I hear on the news, or read in the newspaper, about how "You must make sure your children are reading during the summer so they won't slip behind," I just shake my head. Once a student knows how to read excellently, *there is no slipping behind!*

Go to www.ReadRight.com for more information. You'll face two difficult hurdles: Overcoming your own healthy skepticism and convincing your school district to spend the money. The staff at **Read Right** is extremely supportive. They want you to succeed. I'd wish you luck, but you won't need any. *All you need is a passion for the cause!*

NOTE: Because of the astounding results I've personally witnessed in using Read Right, I truly believe that Read Right is the answer to America's education dilemma.

———— ◆ ————

Never give up on something that you can't go a day without thinking about.
Winston Churchill

CONNECT BY ASSUMING **THE GOLDEN RULE:**

RESPOND RATHER THAN PUNISH

was new to the elementary school. At recess I watched the second, third, and fourth graders swing, play on the monkey bars, and fight for the one ball a student brought to school. What puzzled me was that they had no school balls for everyone to share.

SCENARIO: Fifth Grade Classroom

Ms. J: *Let me ask you kids something. Why is it you don't have any school balls to play with at recess?*

Jill: *The principal took them away because some kids left them out on the playground.*

Sam: *Yeh, now we have to bring our own balls from home.*

Lacey: *And it's too hard to carry them back and forth because they said we couldn't leave them in the classroom overnight.*

Ms. J: *Why not?*

Sam: *Because they are mean and want to punish us!*

Ms. J: *Well, maybe we can do something about that. What if I were able to get some balls and bring them for just our class? Would you all be willing to take care of them?*

James: *But what if someone leaves them out on the playground again?*

Ms. J: *What do you think the consequence should be?*

Jill: *Make that student lose recess for a whole week!*

Sam: *Or take all the balls away for a whole week.*

Ms. J: *Wouldn't that be once again punishing the whole class?*

James: *Well, somebody has to get punished!*

Ms. J: *Why? What good will punishment do?*

Megan: *It will make them be more careful next time.*

Ms. J: *Really? Do you think so? Isn't there a better way to handle this than to punish someone? That's what you were so upset about in the first place.*

Chandler: *So, what would you do?*

Ms. J: *How about if we have a checkout system? A couple of you can be the equipment managers and be responsible for checking out and checking in the balls.*

Lacey: *I'd like to do that. Sam, do you want to do it with me?*

Sam: *Sure. But does that mean we have to go pick up all the balls when the whistle blows? Why do we have to pick up after everyone?*

Ms. J: *You wouldn't have to. You'd have a checklist so you would know who was responsible for checking the ball back in. Do you think that would work?*

Sam: *I guess we could try it. And if that person did it more than once, we wouldn't check the ball out to them again.*

Ms. J: *There you go with the idea of punishment again. Get out your vocabulary journal and let's learn a new word. Write this down: punitive. Do you know what that word means?*

Megan: *It has the same first three letters as punish.*

Ms. J: *Good observation, Megan, and that's what it means—to punish. Now let's also write down this word: responsible. What's the root word?*

Lacey: *Respond.*

Ms. J: *My goodness, we do have such smart students in this class. Yes, Lacey, to respond. Responding to what?*

Chandler: *To what we're supposed to do.*

Ms. J: *Absolutely, Chandler. And what are you supposed to do?*

James: *Take care of the balls that we don't even have? Where are we going to get them? My mom won't let me bring mine to school because she says they'll just get lost or stolen.*

Ms. J: *I'd rather see students learn to be responsible than to just get punished. If we enjoy playing with the balls, wouldn't we want to take care of them?*

Megan: *Okay, Sam and I will be the first equipment managers. Sam, you're the computer geek in the class. You make a schedule for switching off, and I'll make a sign-up sheet. Who wants to take turns taking care of the balls?* [Several hands go up.]

James: *But we still don't have any balls!*

Ms. J: *Let me see what I can do about that. Thank you all for being such good problem solvers.*

That evening during dinner with a friend, I tell him about the situation. Thanks to his generosity, he volunteers to buy balls for the classroom. The next morning as I leave for school, I find on my doorstep two red mesh bags with every different ball you could dream of—two soccer balls, two basketballs, two softballs and bats, two footballs, two kickballs, a tetherball, six hula hoops, six short and two long jump ropes. I am overwhelmed. Attached to the bags is a note that reads:

Dear Fifth Grade Class,

I've been told that you are all responsible students.

I know you'll take good care of this equipment.

Work hard in class and enjoy recess!

From your new Best Ever Friend

Chandler designed a huge thank you note, and all the students added their personal thank you. On the front, it was addressed *To Our New Best-Ever Friend*. For the rest of the year, students took turns being equipment managers. Not once was a ball left out on the playground. None were lost or stolen. None were misused. All students took on, with pride, their individual and collective responsibilities.

What tickled my fancy was how often the students spontaneously used the words *responsible* and *punitive*. They took it to heart. That always puts a smile on my face. Children, like cream, will usually rise to the top when given the opportunity to be reasonable and responsible.

When tempted to use punitive measures, take a step back, breathe deeply, and resolve to make the most of the teachable moment. Ask yourself, does what I am doing push the students away or deepen our connection?

NOTE: Some of you may be wondering if the principal or other teachers inquired as to where all the balls came from, and some suggested that I was undermining the principal's new rule. Yes, the students were asked about the balls; I was asked about the balls. We all just answered that they were donated by Our Best Ever Friend. And what could anyone say to that?

In order to be effective, be responsive. In order to be responsive, listen.
Sharon Weil

CONNECT THROUGH POSITIVE REINFORCEMENT:
CHANGE HABITS & ELIMINATE LABELS

In thirty-five years of teaching, I find it difficult to remember all the acronyms and labels that have been applied to students. Over time, I developed quite an aversion to ADD and ADHD in particular. While there may be some merit in attaching a label to a particular student, it is often unnecessary and unjustified.

I have a fondness in particular for middle and junior high students because of their unlimited energy and because school is their primary focus. At that age, I find it almost amusing that someone would use the ADD/ADHD labels. For goodness sake, most of them are hyperactive, and I say *hurray*. It's not the kid hanging from the chandelier who worries me. Rather, I'm concerned about the kid who sits quietly with little interest in what's happening in or out of the classroom. As an experienced teacher, I know how to harness and redirect energy. Lethargy is a different animal!

SCENARIO 1: [Eighth grader TJ stands at the teacher's desk. He doesn't say anything, just stands there flapping his arms up and down.]

Ms. J: *Yes, TJ. What can I do for you?* [His arms flap up and down almost rhythmically.] *Yes, TJ?*

TJ: *I forgot what I was going to ask you.*

Ms. J: *I can see why. Stand still and focus.*

TJ: *I can't stand still. I'm ADHD.*

Ms. J: *Who told you that?* [Ms. J looks at him quizzically and softens her tone so as not to put him on the defensive.]

TJ: *My special education teacher back in third grade. And my parents. I've always been this way.*

Ms. J: *Well, let's just pretend you're not. Please quit flapping your arms and stand still.*

TJ: *I can't.* [TJ continues flapping his arms.]

Ms. J [smiling]: *I dare you. Stop right now and don't do it anymore. Neither of us can focus on what you're trying to say while you're doing that. So stop.*

[TJ stands with his arms glued to his sides and stares at the teacher.]

Ms. J: *Okay, that's better. Now relax and focus on what you wanted to ask me.*

TJ: *Oh, I remember.* [Continuing to stand still, he brightens.] *My dad wants you to call him. He wants to take me out of school for a couple of days to go on a hunting trip.*

Ms. J: *I'll be happy to give him a call. Thank you for standing still so nice. I knew you could do it.*

I never again saw TJ flap his arms. He just seemed to need permission to have his ADHD label upgraded to *regular student.* That evening when I talked with his dad, I explained what had happened.

Dad: *Yes, that drives us crazy at home. We never did understand the ADHD thing.*

TJ finished the year making A's and B's without any further habitual, or perhaps attention-needing, devices.

NOTE: I can hear some special education teachers and administrators protesting with their justifications for labeling. But sometimes gut instinct and common sense win out. I'm comfortable taking leaps. If it works, great. If not, look for another avenue. But at least give kids a chance to grow out of, or overcome, their labels. You don't always have to buy into all the *education-ese*. Are there students who benefit from professional assistance, i.e., special education, with a focus on certain behavioral challenges? Of course. But be careful about carrying all that too far, especially at an age where *hyperactive* kids are just acting like kids. Junior high is full of kangaroos and squirrels. Accept that and work on focusing all that energy in a positive direction. The gratification will be worth the effort.

If you're gonna make connections which are innovative, you have to not have the same bag of experiences as everyone else does.
Steve Jobs

SCENARIO 2: Scott was an *inclusion* student in my 7th grade reading class. *Inclusion* is a label for special education kids scheduled into a regular classroom. He was slight in build with a wildness in his eyes that made you think he was in a perpetual state of crisis. Scott didn't know how to sit still, to keep from talking out, or to interact appropriately with other students. When he did sit in his desk, he flailed his arms left and right, up and down, striking out, always seeking to touch students around him—perhaps reaching for attention. Needless to say, no one wanted to sit near him. Students complained long and loud about his being a nuisance. I moved Scott's desk a safe distance from the others. A few days into the school year, I asked the special education teacher to think of an excuse to take Scott out of the classroom for a few minutes while I talked with the other students.

Ms. J: *We're going to conduct an experiment, and I need your help. I know you are all irritated that Scott has been assigned to this classroom. However, I want you to know that I believe he is as intelligent as any of you. He just has some bad habits that he needs to overcome. What we're going to do is use positive reinforcement. Research shows that a human being of average intelligence can*

overcome a bad habit within 14 to 21 days if that habit is replaced with something
more positive. Since I believe Scott is above average, just like I believe that about
each of you, we are going to expect him to correct that behavior within only 14
days. That goes for each of you. If you have bad habits, I want you to focus on
changing those within 14 days. For instance, if you are a procrastinator, I can
give you tips on how to fix that for yourself. We'll talk about other habits later.
For now, I want you to give Scott, and me, a chance to work on this. Can I count
on you?

Students roll their eyes, hunch their shoulders, and look dubious.

Ms. J: *I need a show of hands that we'll all give Scott fourteen days.*

Hands were raised, some enthusiastically, some hesitantly, but Ms. J stood there with raised eyebrows until every hand was in the air.

The first few days were challenging. Scott wasn't aware of the plan. As he sat and flailed his arms, Ms. J admonished, *Scott, I'm so glad to see that you are sitting still. You are getting better at it every day.*

Scott looked at the teacher quizzically, like she was nuts. Each day that went by, Ms. J affirmed his good behavior. Students appointed themselves to mark the days on the calendar. Working hard to be encouraging, they even started chiming in, "You're doing better, Scott. I might even want to sit by you soon."

Scott was indeed intelligent. He gradually ceased flailing his arms, began correcting himself when he spoke out of turn, and began smiling when other students gave him praise. Within fourteen days, Scott was an accepted member of the classroom community. Did he slip now and then? Yes, as we all do, but he also grinned widely when he verbalized an apology and corrected his actions.

Not only was that a life-changing experience for Scott, but for the students and teacher as well. If Scott could overcome a label—er, uh, habit—that severe, what could the rest of us do with our bad habits?

NOTE: The aftermath was interesting. Scott's mother *never* did buy into Scott's intelligence or ability to overcome his flailing. She did visit the classroom and was amazed at his appropriate behavior. But she said he continued to be the old *Scott* at home. Ms. J held her tongue to keep from suggesting that he might be behaving as he felt he was expected or allowed to behave. Were all habit-breaking endeavors this successful? Absolutely not. But isn't it worth the effort if you succeed only once or twice? Definitely.

As often as possible, enlist the assistance of your special education team, administrators, and parents. Just don't let wanting their approval be more important than what matters most—the students.

Change the way you look at things, and the things you look at change.
Wayne W. Dyer

SCENARIO 3: Eighth-grade student Emily hardly ever said a word. Ms. J watched her one day coming down the hall toward class. Her head was down, her glasses sliding down her nose, and she walked hunched over the load she was carrying—a notebook with papers sticking out, several books and loose papers piled on top, and pens and pencils clutched tightly in her left hand. As she entered the classroom, she immediately dropped the load on her desk with papers and books falling off onto the floor. She plopped down in her seat and let out a sigh.

Other students nearby rolled their eyes. Ms. J walked up to her.

Ms. J: *Let me help you, Emily.* [Ms. J picks the papers off the floor, hands them to her and touches her lightly on the arm.] *Looks like you're having a rough day. Just relax until the bell rings. I read your short story last night; it's really good. Would you be able to stop by for a few minutes after school today?"*

Ms. J can't tell whether the tears in Emily's eyes are from the compliment, the frustration she feels, or is worried about seeing the teacher after class.

Emily: *Okay, I guess so.*

Emily was the best writer in the class. One of the books she carried every day was a journal of short stories that she worked on every spare moment. Her disorganization was a thorn in her side, as well as that of her other teachers.

Ms. J decides to help Emily with some organization skills so that she can quit frustrating herself and quit feeling the silent and sometimes spoken criticism from other students, teachers, and her parents.

After school, Emily walks into the classroom carrying the same disheveled load.

Ms. J: *Hi, Emily. I called your mom and told her we were going to do a little work together. She's picking you up in about 30 minutes. I hope that's okay with you.*

Emily raises and drops her shoulders as if to say "whatever." She doesn't smile.

Ms. J: *Put your papers and books on that front desk and pull it up here beside mine so we can work together. What I want to do, Emily, is help you get organized so that you'll hopefully experience less frustration in finding things. How does that sound?*

Another shoulder-drop of "whatever."

Ms. J: *Before we start, I want to tell you something. Please understand that I am very sincere when I say that you are an excellent writer. Sometimes when students are totally focused on creative thinking, other things fall by the wayside—like being organized. Let me show you one of my favorite photos. Do you know who this is?*

Emily: *Sure.* [She brightens a bit.] *It's Einstein. He's a genius. Theory of Relativity and all that. I did a report on him for science class last year.*

Ms. J: *That's great. What do you notice about his desk and office?*

Emily: *I guess he just has a lot of stuff he's working on.*

Ms. J: *Yes, you're right. It's kind of a mess, though, isn't it?*

Emily: *I guess so. But his mind is just so busy; he's always working on new theories.* [Emily becomes unusually animated, her eyes widen, and she begins talking faster.] *Did you know he played the violin? Whenever he worked on something he couldn't quite figure out, he played classical music, and then he'd get a big idea from focusing on the music. It was like magic.* [She looks off into the distance as if daydreaming.]

Ms. J: *Are you a musician, Emily?*

Emily: *I play the piano. I've taken piano lessons since first grade. I really do love to practice.*

Ms. J: *Have you studied music theory?*

Emily: *Oh, yes, my teacher is a real stickler for that.*

Ms. J: *Then you probably know a bit about composing—what a composer has to do to come up with a piece of music?*

Emily: *I guess…sort of. I mean, naturally a composer has to follow some rules.*

Ms. J: *Exactly, that's my point. No matter what we are trying to accomplish, it helps to have some guidelines.*

Emily: *I see where you're going with this. You want me to get organized. My mom and dad preach at me all the time about that.* [She wears a look of guilt.]

Ms. J: *That's what I want to help you with. The first thing we want to do is take everything off your desk except your notebook. Just set your papers and books on the corner of my desk.*

Ms. J gives Emily dividers, helps her tab the sections, then clip all of her loose papers in the proper places. They include a tab for *Writing Ideas*. In the front of the notebook, they clip in a clear, zippered pocket for holding pens, pencils, protractor, etc., and a planner/calendar for writing down all of the assignments and appointments. Ms. J shows Emily how to double-stack her books on top of her notebook so she can carry them with ease. Ms. J then picks up the notebook, puts two books side by side on top, then adds another stack on top of that. Holding the notebook and the four stacked books in front, Ms. J walks across the room and back.

Ms. J: *There, you try it now, Emily. Stand up straight so you don't have all the weight in front of you.*

Emily, looking rather self-conscious, slowly gets up from her desk. She picks up the notebook with books on top and walks across the room.

Ms. J: *Shoulders back, Emily.* [Ms. J smiles encouragingly as Emily straightens her back.] *You know, my mother used to make me practice walking across the room with a book on my head because she said it would keep me from slouching. Want to try it, just for fun?* [Ms. J picks up a large book, sets it on her head, and proceeds across the room without the book slipping.]

Emily [laughing]. *Really? Do you practice that?*

Ms. J: *Well, not so much, but once in a while just to keep good posture. Try it.*

Emily picks up a dictionary, sets it on her head, and takes two steps before it slips off.

Emily: *This is harder than it looks.* [She sets the book back on her head, straightens her shoulders, and walks cautiously across the room.]

Ms. J [clapping]: *That was great! You did it! Do you think you can practice that at home?*

Emily [smiling]: *Oh, yes. I'll do it every day right after I practice my piano. That way I won't forget.*

Just then Emily's mother walks into the room.

Mom: *Ready to go, Hon? Your brother is waiting in the car.*

Emily: *Oh, mom, I can't wait to show you my notebook that's all organized, and how I'm learning to have good posture.*

Mom: *I can hardly wait. Thanks, Ms. J. for taking the time. We really appreciate it.*

Ms. J: *My pleasure to work with such a stellar student. She's a quick study. See you tomorrow, Emily.*

NOTE: Emily entered class every day with a smile and interacted with other students who came to appreciate her talents. Sometimes a loose paper was sticking out here or there, but she continued to improve and was quite happy with herself. She was no longer labeled by others, or herself, as disorganized and messy. Her mom reported that she even started keeping her room neat and had the entire family laughing as they challenged each other with bigger and bigger books to balance on their heads. Emily won a writing competition near the end of her 8th grade year and was published in a teen anthology.

SCENARIO 4: Eighth Grade Language Arts. Jackson was the class clown and had been since kindergarten.

Ms. J: *Excuse me, Class, I need to interrupt our discussion here. Jackson, you seem to have something to add to what each of us is expressing. I appreciate your wit, but it has become interruptive. I'll make you a deal. If you will give your full attention to the class and me and speak up only when you have something that contributes positively to the discussion, I'll give you fifteen minutes each Friday to be on stage.*

Jackson: *What do you mean? What do you want me to do?*

Ms. J: *You seem to have a knack for being funny. Just be yourself. Entertain us with a comedy routine.*

Jackson: *I can do that. No problem. When do I start?*

Ms. J: *This is Monday. You have all week to prepare. Be ready on time and fill in the entire fifteen minutes. That's the deal. Shake?*

Jackson, grinning broadly, standing tall with shoulders back, approaches Ms. J and shakes her hand. He saunters proudly back to his seat. Students look from him to the teacher in disbelief.

Friday. Ms. J takes a seat with the students and waits. Jackson enters with a portable tape recorder and microphone.

Jackson: *Hello, Ladies and Gentlemen. I am here today to interview you. Get that gray matter cranked up, and remember, you're being recorded so I want some real jazzy comments.*

Jackson, approaching each student, asks them questions and has a witty response to each. He goes overtime just a bit. Ms. J is in awe of his confidence and ability to think fast on his feet. The class applauds, and he takes his seat. He keeps his word at being a productive part of the class.

The following Friday and the one after that, Jackson regales the class with a stand-up comedy routine, a one-man skit, and always finishes on time. The students and Ms. J all enjoy Jackson's performance. By the fourth Friday, Jackson's routine is only five minutes long.

Jackson comes into the classroom before school. *Could I talk to you, Ms. J?*

Ms. J: *Sure, Jackson, what's up?*

Jackson: *I don't want to do the Friday thing anymore. I just can't think of something new every week.*

Ms. J: *Well, okay then, but I still need your cooperation. What about that?*

Jackson: *I'm sorry. Sometimes I get carried away. I think of funny things to say, puns and stuff, and I guess sometimes I don't know how to do it respectfully. I'll do better, honest.*

Ms. J: *I appreciate your sincerity, Jackson. I'll find a way to smooth it over with the class so they don't think you bailed. You know, Jackson, you really are very talented. Are you familiar with the famous comedian, Robin Williams? You remind me of him. Spontaneous, witty, bright. I'd like to suggest that you go to the charter school next year that focuses on performing arts.*

Jackson: *Really? You mean a school like the movie "Fame"?*

Ms. J: *Yes, exactly like that. You'll still have to do school work, but you'll have a chance to use your natural talents. Would you like for me to talk to your parents about this?*

Jackson: *Gosh, that would be great. Thanks, Ms. J. And I'm going to be the best student in the class from now on.*

That's all it took—some personal attention without criticism. Find the strengths of each student and build on those.

———— ◆ ————

Do not train a child to learn by force or harshness; but direct them to it by what amuses their minds, so that you may be better able to discover with accuracy the peculiar bent of the genius of each.

Plato

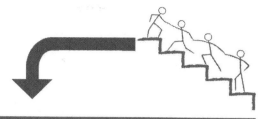

CONNECT TO SUCCESS:
BE PATIENT AND PERSEVERE

Based on my varied experience, the School District hired me to do something with the junior high students who weren't succeeding. In the interview, I asked, "What is the curriculum?"

The Director answered, "Whatever you want it to be. Just do something with these kids. We've got to get them out of regular classrooms so other kids can learn. We're basically hiring you to relieve the teachers of negative students."

Undaunted, I gleefully, and naively, accepted the position. Develop my own curriculum to help kids in trouble? No problem! The teachers cleaned out their classrooms, happily reassigning to me anyone getting less than a "C" grade and/or causing disruption.

The first day went like this:

Bernice. straddled her chair, sitting with her back to me. She wore, like badges of honor, a black leather jacket, skull-and-cross-bone dangly earrings, and black leather pants. She was a beautiful girl with gorgeous honey-blonde hair.

I said to myself, *Give her time. She'll come around.* To her I said, *Bernice, please turn around and give me your attention.*

Bernice looked at me over her shoulder. In her cold, sultry voice, she responded, "There. I've given you my attention. Happy now?"

I smiled to myself. *Yes, she'll come around. Be patient.*

Student #1: *So we're here because we're stupid, right?*

Student #2: *What are we going to do in here? How is this going to work?*

Student #3: *I really like your fingernail polish. What color is that?*

Student #4: *Do we have to do real work in here or are you gonna play shrink?*

I asked the students to fill out a survey with questions like: What's your favorite number; what's your favorite color; if you could be a flavor of ice cream, what would it be; would you rather be a giraffe, a monkey, or a tiger? How do you feel about being kicked out of class because you are not making good grades? What do you want to do with your life? How do you feel about failing? How do you feel about succeeding?

The students quietly, and to my surprise, seemed to take the survey seriously. The comment section at the end of the survey said: *Write something about you that you think I should know. Don't share anything your parents wouldn't want you to share.*

That night I pored over the surveys. The first several questions were my way of connecting with kids. The comment sections ranged from cautious to shocking:

- I wish my mom would let me grow my hair long.
- I hate the music teacher; she always embarrasses me in front of the class.
- The other kids think I'm weird because I have a pet boa constrictor.
- Sometimes my stepdad comes home drunk and makes me sleep outside, so I crawl in with my big dog to keep warm.
- I don't know where my parents are. I live with the guy who found me sleeping in a dumpster. He's okay. But I miss my mom and dad.

- I'm Haida Indian. Okay? So, don't think I'm gonna like a white-___ teacher!
- I can't read or write so don't make me do no work.

The principal was supportive in giving me a budget. I decided to call the class *Success Class*. I purchased for each student a copy of the paperback *The Greatest Salesman in the World* by Og Mandino.* At the beginning of the class, I passed out the books, telling the students to write their names in their books but leave them in the classroom each day at the end of the period.

I began reading the story as each student in their own way followed along. We often stopped for new vocabulary. Skipping the middle section of the chapters explaining *The Scrolls,* we finished the story. I could tell students were curious, and some touched by the ending. Going back then to the chapters containing *The Scrolls,* we began learning the success principles of each. As instructed in the book, we read the first chapter every day for two weeks before moving onto the next chapter. We memorized and repeated each day, the essence of each scroll:

1. *Today I begin a new life.*
2. *I will greet this day with love in my heart.*
3. *I will persist until I succeed.*
4. *I am nature's greatest miracle.*
5. *I will live this day as if it is my last.*
6. *I am master of my emotions.*
7. *I will laugh at the world for this too shall pass.*
8. *I will multiply my value a hundredfold.*
9. *I will act now.*
10. *I will ask for guidance.*

---

*Mandino, Og. *The Greatest Salesman in the World.* New York, NY: Bantam Books, Inc., 1983.

Students were intrigued, curious, doubtful, and somewhere on a spectrum from totally hungry for success to terrified of success. I pressed on. I vacillated from being gratified at their attention to being totally discouraged that I wasn't making any headway. About November of that year, a colleague asked how it was going. Sensing my frustration and discouragement, he gave me these words of wisdom:

Write in your calendar on March 15, "See, it's all better now." So, I did just that.

A few weeks into the class, Jonah came in clenching his teeth and his fists. Picking up a chair, he hurled it across the room. No one was hurt; neither were the students shocked. They were used to his tantrums. Jonah looked at me, waiting for a reaction.

Ms. J, calmly: *So, Jonah, why are you so angry today?*

Jonah: *I'm tired of everyone trying to make me white. I'm not white, and I don't wanna be white.*

Ms. J: *Okay, so what are you? What do you want to be?*

Jonah: *I'm Haida. I'm dark. My hair is black. My eyes are black. Don't you see that?*

Ms. J: *Okay, Jonah. I'm not from here. I don't know Haida. Tell me what it is.*

Jonah: *Gee, Teach. You don't know Haida? It's Indian, that's what. I thought teachers were supposed to know stuff.*

Ms. J: *Well, I'm sorry. I'm Indian, too, but my Indian is from the Southeast part of the United States.*

Jonah: *You're not Indian. You don't look Indian. You look white.*

Ms. J: *I confess—I'm only half Indian. Choctaw. Ever heard of them?*

Jonah: *No.*

Ms. J: *Well, gee, Jonah, we're even then. You tell me about Haida, and I'll tell you about Choctaw. Deal?*

Jonah, hanging his head reluctantly: *Yeh, I guess so.*

During this dialogue, the students sat quietly, looking at each other like *How's all this going to shake out?*

Ms. J: *For now, Jonah, let's get on with class, and you and I will work out our Indian-ness later. I'll get back to you with a plan.* He sat down and was quiet for the rest of the class period.

I arranged with the principal and parents to take Jonah to a bookstore that specialized in all things Native American. Ahead of time, I called the proprietor and told him the situation. He was excited. The principal covered my afternoon classes. (Exceptionally nice support!) I introduced Jonah to the bookstore owner who took over from there. The next three hours were spent looking at books covering Haida art, history, and music. The bookstore owner generously gifted three books to Jonah. Two weeks later, Jonah asked if he could do a presentation in front of the class. He dressed in Haida costume, played music on a CD, showed Haida masks that he had made himself, and told in story form the history of the Haida people. What a learning experience for all of us. Best of all, having claimed his identity and shared it with others, Jonah relaxed into being a stellar student.

Back to Bernice—She was holding out, not wanting to give in to my expectations. Without calling her out, I decided to take some time just to see what pet peeves students had about school in general. Bernice was the first to speak up.

Bernice: *What bugs me is that some students are so uppity just because they make good grades. I've tried really hard, but I'm just not an A student. There ought to be some kind of recognition for students who at least try and do a little better.*

Ms. J: *Like what kind of recognition do you mean?*

Bernice: *Every year they have an assembly for those students who make the honor roll. But some of us will never get up that high with our GPA. And then those same kids get to be honored at the end of the year with certificates and trophies; it's always the same kids getting honored. It's just not fair.*

Ms. J: *You know, Bernice, I think you've made a good point. What do you think we should do about that?*

Bernice's eyes widen: *I don't know exactly. Just something.*

Ms. J: *How many of you feel the same way?*

All hands go up.

Ms. J: *Okay, then. Raise your hand if you want to be on a committee to change this situation.*

A dozen hands go up. I ask Bernice to write down the names. We set a time later that week to meet after school, and Bernice clears it with the principal. She is not the least intimidated and lets me know the plan.

The committee decides to start a program called **Be a PAL**. Bernice comes up with the acronym: **PAL: Progressive Achievement League.** Each student who raises their grade point average at least .3 (three-tenths of one percent) in one quarter is invited to join **PAL**. Bernice even gets the principal to spring for certificates and a pizza party at the end of each quarter for those students. The enthusiasm spreads like wildfire. The committee, now calling themselves *The PAL Council*, enlists the help of the district technology guru to write a program that calculates who earns .3 improvement. Invitations are then sent to each student who qualifies, and certificates are printed. The Council makes buttons that students wear proudly. By the end of the school year, 89 percent of the student body belongs to **PAL**. The last day of school, Bernice comes in to see me.

Bernice: *Ms. J, I want to thank you for all you've done for the other PAL kids and me. It's been a great year.*

Ms. J: *It's been my pleasure, Bernice, to see your progress. I am so proud of you. In fact, you're not far from being in the Honor Society yourself, right?*

Bernice: *Yes, I'm getting there. What I want to do now, though, is take PAL to all the other junior highs.*

Ms. J: *Wow! That's quite an idea. How do you propose to do that?*

Bernice: *That's where I need your help. During the summer, I want to go talk to the other five principals in the district so we can have it up and running when school starts. Will you go with me?*

Ms. J: *You make the appointments, and I'll be glad to go.*

Long story short, **PAL** became a part of every junior high with a parent volunteer as an advisor at each school. Bernice made a video explaining the program and presented it at a school board meeting with an astoundingly articulate explanation. Then she and I presented it at a state education convention. We had more responses from teachers all over the country than we could handle that next year. I've always wondered how far and wide **PAL** blossomed because of one student's idea to change the lives of thousands of junior high kids.

AN ASIDE: When I flipped the calendar to March that spring, I had to smile. Yes, it was all better now, just as my colleague had assured me it would be. Those words, *See, it's all better now*, have gotten me through many challenges since then. Growth—the students' as well as mine—takes time, patience, support, and perseverance.

———— ◆ ————

It's not the job of the teacher to save a child's soul; it is the teacher's job to provide an opportunity for the child to save his or her own soul.
Rafe Esquith

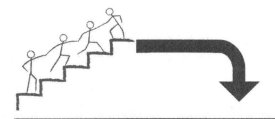

CONNECT THROUGH TEACHABLE MOMENTS:
TURN NEGATIVES INTO OPPORTUNITIES

We've all been there. Some student commits an unforgivable atrocity inside the classroom, and we all have to stay in from recess until the culprit confesses. How about we all agree to not make such a big deal out of kids being kids? I'm not talking about bullying or more serious offenses.

Students are young people with sometimes not much experience at making the best decisions. Take every opportunity to allow students to apologize for behavior without losing face.

SCENARIO 1: Last day of school. 4th Grade Classroom. The teacher needs to go to the office and leaves the class unattended. By the way, in most states, leaving students unattended is a serious violation by the teacher.

Teacher: *I have to leave the room. Do not get out of your seats. I repeat: No one is to get out of their seats while I am out of the room.*

Johnny reaches over to Janet's desk, takes her pencil box and tosses it to another student who proceeds to fling it into the corner. Janet gets up from her desk and retrieves the pencil box. A few minutes later, the teacher re-enters the room.

Teacher: *Did anyone get out of their desks while I was gone?*

Johnny: *Janet did!* [Students snicker.]

Teacher: *Janet, you will stay fifteen minutes after school.*

Janet: *But they…*

Teacher: *I don't want to hear it. Not another word out of you, young lady.*

Remember, this was the last day of school. The bell rings. Janet is the first one out the door and glad to be rid of such an unreasonable teacher. By the way, I was that student in that 4th grade classroom. This situation was burned on my brain as a teachable moment for me when I became a teacher.

NOTE: The teacher, first of all, should not have left the class unattended. Secondly, the demand to stay in their seats was unreasonable. What about an emergency? The teacher set up an untenable situation. A simple solution upon re-entering and seeing all students sitting in their seats would be to NOT ask if anyone disobeyed. Instead, wish the students a happy summer and let it go at that. If someone tattled on Janet without being asked, the matter could simply have been settled by asking her to remain after class, hearing her side of the story, and letting her get on her way with warm wishes for a happy summer.

SCENARIO 2: The new principal has laid down the law. No hats in school. Two seniors decide to test the new principal as well as the new English teacher. They both walk into the classroom wearing very large cowboy hats. They take their seats in the middle of the room.

Ms. J: *Excuse me, gentlemen, would you mind sitting in the back of the classroom. I'm afraid your hats will get in the way of someone else seeing.*

The two seniors look at each other, get up quietly, and sit in the back row. The next day, they are not wearing their hats.

NOTE: Use every opportunity to de-escalate a situation. Kids are going to push the limits. Don't push back. Find a way around them and help them save face. In fact, *saving face* is essential to young people whose self-esteem is on the line every moment of every day. The teacher's job is to help students grow at every opportunity. Watch carefully and take advantage of those timely lessons.

SCENARIO 3: Seventh grader, Kenny, is from a wealthy family. He gets his kicks from intimidating other students. He's used to getting his way, ordering other students around, reminding them of who his father is and their status in the small town.

Kenny: *Hey, I had $200 in my wallet, and now it's gone. Who took it?*

NOTE: Do not go on a search for the wallet; do not question the class; do not look for a culprit. The teacher has only one appropriate response in this case. Take Kenny aside and explain to him, *I'm sorry your wallet with the money is missing. However, as it states in your student handbook, you are advised not to bring large amounts of money to school. If you need to pay for something substantial, you should check the money into the office upon arrival. As soon as class is over, you need to go to the office to report the missing items. Now, please take your seat, and we'll get back to the lesson.*

Do not allow him to protest further. Also, do not allow him to go to the office during class. If you do, you are setting a precedent for his knowing how to ditch class in the future. Don't fall for his scheme. Be prepared to hear from the parents. They, too, may be used to flaunting their status and getting their way. Explain the situation to the administration at your first opportunity so they can be prepared to back you up if or when the parents call.

This scenario is not intended to show prejudice against rich students. While confronting the situation, be sure to measure your tone with compassion. This student is as much a victim of his circumstances as the less fortunate student.

Kids react like they are taught and/or allowed to react. It's the adults in their lives who have made this situation possible; don't blame the student. Remember to look for ways to make this a teachable moment.

———— ◆ ————

A wise teacher does not react to situations
without carefully considering the options.
RJW

MORE TEACHABLE MOMENTS:
PASSING NOTES AND FINDING NOTES

If you see students passing notes, decide if you can look away, i.e., ignore them. They are kids; they are in school. Of course they are going to pass notes.

If note-passing happens during a test, you have to put a stop to it. The question then becomes *Are you going to read it?* That possibly puts you in a position of finding out that they are cheating on the test, and you'll have to address that. If the note indeed reveals cheating, put a red mark on that particular question(s) on the test paper of each student involved, and admonish them with a note, "Cheating is wrong; stop doing it." If you decide not to read the note, or if the note has nothing to do with the test, pull the culprits aside and explain how it might appear to someone looking on.

If you find a note on the floor or lying about after students leave the classroom, read it. If it's a witchy drawing of you, tear it up and forget it. If it's a note that needs follow-up, e.g., something detrimental to a student, then, by all means, follow it up with an administrator, counselor, or parent. But be sure it is serious enough to follow up. Otherwise, toss the note and forget it.

Most student-written notes are harmless. Don't pounce on kids for sharing their ideas and feelings with a friend. Be glad they are engaged in written communication.

———◆———

We all–most of us, anyway–want connections with other
people and spend our lives looking for them.
Paul Auster

CONNECT WITH THE MOST UNLIKELY:

MOTIVATE WITH RECOGNITION

Remember Scott, the student who had a habit of wanting attention by striking out at other students?

SCENARIO: The seventh graders are reading aloud T.S. Eliot's *Cats* poetry— Broadway play lyrics adapted as a Readers' Theatre.

Carol: *Hey, Ms. J, do you think we could put on this play and invite our parents?*

Ms. J: *What a great idea! It will take a whole lot of work. Anyone else interested?*

Students look at each other dubiously.

Carol: *Come on, guys. It will be fun.*

Mark: *You mean we'd have to memorize the whole thing?*

Ms. J: *Actually, we could read it with scripts, just like we're doing now.*

Bruce: *That will look really dumb. Who would want to watch us do that?*

Margie: If we had costumes, it would be really cool.

Ms. J's head starts spinning—costumes, scenery, rehearsals—Pandora's box....

Carol: Could we, Ms. J, pleeease?

Ms. J: *Well, let's see...how many are interested?*

All of the girls raised their hands but only a smattering of boys.

Ms. J: *Let me make some phone calls to see if we can get some parent help. I'll get back to you.*

That evening Ms. J called two of the parents who had signed up to be classroom volunteers. They agreed to do all the costumes. *No problem; leave it to us!* The next morning Ms. J approached the art teacher and explained what the students wanted to do. *Fantastic! I'd love to help. We'll make it our next quarter's project.* At lunchtime, Ms. J explained the idea to the band and choir teachers. *What a great idea! I can write a score for the band to play in between the readings.* The choir teacher was a bit hesitant. *We're practicing for contest, but the choir could learn a couple of songs, and maybe a finale. Would that work?*

Ms. J was astonished at the willingness of all the participants. Her biggest challenge was turning all of that over to others. Would they do it the way she would want it? Or could she just let go and trust? Since time was of the essence, she chose the latter.

Motivation in the classroom was at an all-time high. The students vied for parts, wrangled a bit, and settled on who was best for each Cat...except Scott who wanted a main part.

Jeff: *Scott can't do it. He can barely read.*

Scott: *That's not true. I can so read.*

Carol: *I think we should let him try it.*

Scott: *Thanks, Carol.*

Ms. J: *Does anyone else want that part? How about you, Jeff?*

Jeff: *Are you kiddin' me? That's too many lines.*

Carol: *Then don't put Scott down if you don't want it.*

Ms. J: *Since no one else wants it, the part is yours, Scott. I know you can do it.*

The girls, all jumping up and down, clapped in excitement. The boys rolled their eyes at each other.

A few days before the performance, Scott's mother called.

Mom: *I don't know what you're thinking. Scott will weasel out. He never follows through on anything.*

Ms. J: *Oh, my. He is so eager to read the part. He's been practicing and seems quite confident.*

Mom: *You don't know Scott. He'll panic at the last minute and let everyone down.*

Ms. J: *I'm sorry to hear you feel that way. At this point, I don't think we can make a change. I'd like to give him the chance to see it through. It's okay if he makes mistakes. Everyone will understand.*

Mom: *I don't want to be embarrassed. If it doesn't go well, it's on you.*

Ms. J: *That's fine. I appreciate your calling.* [Click] Ms. J, as determined as Scott, said aloud to herself, *No way am I letting Scott down at this late date. I think he's going to do just fine.*

Parents bought each Cat student a pair of sweats and decorated each with fur to match the character they portrayed. The cheerleaders painted the faces of the Cats. The art department created a magnificent city night-scene of skyscrapers with Christmas lights for windows. They also created a steam engine with the 7th graders twirling umbrellas for the locomotive wheels as they wound through the audience. The band members played beautifully. The choir performed a moving rendition of "Memory" as the finale. Over four hundred people were in attendance.

At the end of the performance, the students took their bows. Scott grinned from whisker to whisker as he took his bow. Ms. J handed out *KitKat* candy bars to all the performers and students who helped. As she turned to leave the stage, Scott walked up to her accompanied by his mother. She was in tears.

Ms. J: *I'm so proud of you, Scott. Your performance was flawless.*

Scott: *Ms. J, I just want to thank you for letting me have a big part. I know I did a super job. This is the most important thing I have ever done in my life. I'll never forget it.*

Ms. J, holding back tears, gives Scott a big hug.

Mom: *I don't know what to say, except, thank you for believing in Scott. I'm so proud of him.*

Scott, a big grin on his face: *Can I have another KitKat? I think I earned it!*

Ms. J: *Here—you may have all that's left. Just don't eat them all at once.*

Scott: *Cool! Thanks, Ms. J…*and off he skipped.

NOTE: Keep in mind that recognition is one of the highest motivating factors. If students feel they can't get recognition for succeeding in school, they will try for negative recognition. Show students that negative behavior has consequences. Positive behavior earns them positive recognition. Genuine, sincere praise for small or large efforts is appreciated by everyone. Make sure it's just that—well-earned and sincere. Kids can smell false praise like an animal can smell fear. And one more thing, Ms. J did indeed learn to turn over the responsibilities to others, to include them in the production, to work as a team instead of doing it all herself. Teamwork. What a gratifying experience for everyone.

———— ◆ ————

I am not a teacher, but an awakener.

Robert Frost

CONNECT BY SETTING THE MOOD:

BRING JOY TO THE CLASSROOM

Music class, especially in elementary school, should be fun as well as informative. On this particular morning, Ms. J is covering for the music teacher. The third graders are a delight—all except for Shelby, aka Little Miss Cranky Pants. At the beginning of each class, Ms. J writes her name on the board along with the word *JOY*. She draws a face in the word *JOY* with eyes, eyelashes, nose, and smiling mouth, then turns to the students, introduces herself, and says, *I wish you joy!*

If anything occurs that drains her joy, she stops the class and says, *I wish you joy. Can you wish each other that and me as well?* Each turns and says to the other, *I wish you joy.* In addition, elementary students are often big on tattling. As long as someone is not in serious pain or being harmed in any way, Ms. J tells them to turn to the person who is bugging them and say, *I wish you joy.* Works like a charm with elementary students and resolves the situation.

But the scowl on the face of Shelby seems permanent—the furrowed brow, the downturned mouth, the hands-on-hips, directing and demanding to have her way. The students are using the *I wish you joy* with each other in an effective way, but Little Miss Cranky Pants doesn't want to give up her negative territory while the other kids are all singing and dancing in a circle to *The Farmer in the Dell.*

Shelby demands, *I am the cheese. The cheese stands alone. Get out of my circle.* Ms. J stops the music and requires everyone to stand still and be silent. She approaches Shelby and kneels down to look her in the eyes. Touching her lightly on her forearm, Ms. J says *You seem to be a little out of sorts today. I need for you to change your mind and have joy. I wish you joy today.* Ms. J then turns to all the other children. *Let's all wish Shelby joy until she changes her mind.* Shelby's scowl deepens as she hangs her head, eyes downcast. The students all chime in as a chorus *We wish you joy.* Brow, still furrowed, Shelby looks out at the group. Ms. J holds her hand. The class repeats, *We wish you joy.* Shelby's brow relaxes. *We wish you joy.* Her downturned mouth turns into a half-smile. *We wish you joy.* She gives a little laugh. Ms. J gives her a hug and tells her she'll have to wait her turn to be chosen as the cheese. Smiling, Shelby joins the circle. Ms. J resumes the music.

All goes well. The kids sing, circle around, and Shelby is indeed chosen as the cheese the next time around. Five minutes before class is over, Ms. J plays a CD of *The Blue Danube* and lets the students have free-dance. The mood is joy-full as they, without any inhibition, dance and twirl around the room.

Time to line up, Kids. Shelby runs over to Ms. J, looks up at her, smiles sweetly, and says, *I wish you joy.* Ms. J gives her a hug and responds, *Thank-you, and I wish you joy all day long.*

NOTE: I introduce myself this same way in middle school and high school. The challenge is to maintain my JOY when challenged by students who tower over me or students who have so much pain in their lives that they don't believe anyone cares enough to truly wish them joy. I then turn up my resolve several notches, put a smile on my face, and relax my shoulders.

Only once did this seem to go awry. One day as I answered a call from the principal, I turned around to find my JOY face turned into graffiti. I simply said, *Oh, that's creative.* Then I re-drew the JOY face next to the graffiti, smiled, and said *I wish you joy.* Students squirmed a bit, looked sheepish, some smiled. We resumed class without further incident. How you, the teacher, handle the situation is, most of the time, a simple choice, a simple resolution, a simple JOY.

———— ♦ ————

When we ground ourselves in the present moment, we spontaneously connect better with others. We become more responsive and less reactive, listening more deeply and speaking with greater clarity.
Lama Surya Das

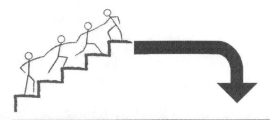

CONNECT WITH THE MARGINALIZED:
ADVOCATE FOR STUDENTS

SCENARIO: Junior High--Casting for the All-School Play

Trina: *But Ms. J, he's a loser. We don't want Philip in the play.*

Ms. J: *Wait a minute, Kids. We have a rule that there is a part to play by anyone who wants to participate in what is rightfully called the all-school play. That's my philosophy. Every junior high student gets a chance.*

Quincy: *But he'll mess up. You'll see. He'll miss rehearsals; he won't learn his lines. He'll ruin it for all of us. He always does.*

Ms. J: *That may be. But we're going to let him decide that. I expect each of you to be supportive. Got it?* Grumbling, the two students shook their heads and walked off with sagging shoulders.

After-school rehearsals for the next two weeks were intense. While most students learned their own parts as well as most of the others', Philip had to be prompted with every-other line.

Ms. J took him aside. *So, what's up, Philip? Do you have a hard time memorizing? I can help you with that if you want to make time.*

Philip looked at the ground and shuffled from one foot to the other. *I'm sorry, Ms. J. I've just been real busy, and I just haven't had time to work on the script.*

Ms. J: *Look, Philip, let's cut to the chase. You know how the other kids feel about your being here. They don't believe you can handle it. But I believe in you. I want you to show them, your parents, and the rest of the student body that you can succeed. How can I help you do that?*

Philip: *Thanks, Ms. J. I really do appreciate it. I'll work real hard tonight and this weekend, and I'll know my part by Monday. I promise.*

Monday rehearsal.

Ms. J: *Where's Philip? Has anyone seen him?*

Quincy: *Oh, guess what, Ms. J. He was absent today. I heard he went skiing with his older brother. Ask us if we're surprised!*

Ms. J, disappointed, thought to herself… *How am I going to help Philip if he can't keep his promise for even a few days? I so badly want him to succeed—for several reasons. The students need to see that believing in someone gives them the power to succeed. And Philip needs this.*

Philip, the son of a popular city councilman, was known among the faculty as a latch-key kid. In fact, the neighbors had him over for supper more than he was ever home. Everyone felt sorry for him. His grades, attitude, and behavior were less than acceptable. Ms. J desperately wanted to see him succeed in this one thing that he had chosen for himself.

Tuesday rehearsal.

Ms. J: *Hello, Philip. We missed you yesterday at rehearsal. You know our policy about missing rehearsals. Was it an emergency?*

Philip couldn't make eye contact. *I'm sorry, Ms. J, but my brother was home from college, and he wanted to take me skiing, and I never get to be with him, and…well…I just didn't think this one time would hurt anything.*

Ms. J: *You've let the cast down, Philip, but we can forgive one time. Do I have your commitment that you'll be here every rehearsal from now on and learn your lines?*

Philip: *Thanks, Ms. J, I won't let you down again. I promise.*

Wednesday rehearsal.

Trina: *Ms. J, we've had it with Philip. He doesn't know any of his lines, and he keeps messing up, and he doesn't know his entrances and exits…*

Ms. J: *Okay, okay. I get the picture. I'll see what I can do.*

While the cast was cleaning up, Ms. J approached the errant member. *Philip, stay after rehearsal, please. We need to talk. What's going on here? I've given you multiple chances, the other students are counting on you, and I don't see you keeping your promise. What gives?*

Philip: *I've never been in a play before, Ms. J, and I just wanted to be part of the group. They all have such a good time together, and I wanted to go out to the Dairy Queen with them afterward, but they're all mad at me.*

Ms. J: *This is the first play for many of the students. What do you expect, Philip? They're all doing their parts; you've let them down more than once.*

Philip: *Well, it isn't as if my part is very important. It's just a few lines.*

Ms. J: *Philip, remember what I said at the beginning. Everyone in this play is as important as the next person. If we don't have your lines, your character, we have a big hole in the story. We need you to perform your very best. I want you to succeed at this, Philip. Tomorrow morning, I want you in my classroom thirty minutes before school starts. We're going to work on your lines. Understood?*

Philip: *Thanks, Ms. J. I appreciate it. I'll be there for sure.*

Thursday morning.

Ms. J: *Hey there, Philip. Glad to see you on time. Now let's get down to business and learn these lines. It will be fun to surprise the rest of the cast this afternoon, won't it?*

Philip worked hard. He learned the lines quickly. That afternoon, Philip did indeed surprise the rest of the cast with his attention, knowing his lines, entering and exiting on cue. Ms. J crossed her fingers; the cast gave a collective sigh of relief. All went well the remaining weeks of rehearsal. Philip seemed very proud of himself and was invited to join the cast after rehearsals at their favorite DQ hangout.

Opening night. The performance was flawless…until Philip's cue for entering. The cast member repeated the cue. No Philip. The silence was deafening. Ms. J looked around for Philip's parents in the audience but couldn't spot them. She hurried backstage to determine the problem. Susan, the student stage manager, shook her head in disbelief.

Susan: *He was here earlier, Ms. J. I don't know what happened to him.*

Ms. J: *Grab one of the other cast members, quickly, stick a hat on his head and send him out there.*

After the play, Laura, the principal, approached Ms. J. *Where did Philip disappear to tonight, Ms. J? Is there a problem I need to be aware of? I saw him here earlier.*

Ms. J: *Laura, you know the problem better than I do. I don't know where he went or why. He was doing so well, and we all counted on him to keep his promise. I'm very worried about him. By the way, I didn't see his parents in the audience.*

Laura: *They weren't here. His dad was giving a party at their house for one of the election candidates. But that's not surprising. They've never been ones to attend school activities involving their kids. I'm sure you knew that.*

Ms. J: *Yes, well, I thought this time might be different. Philip really has worked hard to be successful this time. I'm sorry for him, Laura.*

Laura: *I'll make some calls and see what I can find out. I hope he's okay. It puts the school in a precarious position since he was here earlier this evening.*

Next day, before school, Philip dragged into my classroom.

Philip: *The principal sent me down to apologize for cutting out last night.*

Ms. J: *Philip, I'm glad you're okay. We were all worried about you.*

Philip: *Are you mad at me?*

Ms. J: *Mad? No, nothing you could ever do would make me mad. I am disappointed, and so are all the other cast members. Do you want to explain?*

Philip: *I was all ready to play my part. And I was nervous and excited. But I peeked out from behind the curtains. My mom said she'd be there. My dad was at a party, but she said she'd be there, and I didn't see her, and I knew she wouldn't keep her promise and come, and I got so mad that I just left. They're always letting me down.*

Ms. J: *Where did you go, Philip?*

Philip: *I just went down to the DQ and hung out. I just couldn't go on stage. I was so upset. And I'm sorry I let everyone down, but...*

Philip broke into tears, sat down in a desk, and put his head on his arms, his shoulders heaving with sobs.

Ms. J put her hand on his shoulder. *Philip, I'm so sorry. We counted on you, and you let us down. You counted on your mother, and she let you down. Do you see how broken promises have a kind of domino effect? I want you to know that we got through the play. The kids did a wonderful job, and probably only a few noticed that we had a little glitch when we had to substitute for your part. Life happens, Philip, and sometimes we just have to make the best of it. But I'll tell you what. The sky didn't really fall in; it just felt like it did for you last night. I'm so sorry you were disappointed. The big question is: How are you going to let this affect you?*

Philip: *Wh..what d..d..do you mean?* Philip gasped between sobs, trying to dry his tears on his shirt sleeve. Ms. J handed him a tissue.

Ms. J: *Philip, I have said this at every rehearsal, and now I think you'll understand what it means. In every adversity is a seed of success. Do you understand what adversity means?"*

Philip: *Yeh, I guess so. It means when bad things happen to you.*

Ms. J: *That's right. Your parents let you down. And you let us down. It was an adversity but not the end of the world. It's a seed. Now, what are you supposed to do with a seed?*

Philip sighed: *Plant it.*

Ms. J: *That's right. And it will grow into something beautiful. What do you want this to grow into, Philip? This may all sound kind of corny, pardon the pun, but how can you turn this difficult situation into a success?*

Philip: *I don't know, Ms. J, but I promise I'll think about it. And I'm really sorry. Are all the kids mad at me?*

Ms. J: *Yes, I suppose they are, Philip. How do you want to handle that?*

Philip: *I guess I could write them an apology, but I don't want to go to the cast party. I don't deserve that.*

Ms. J: *No, Philip, you probably don't deserve to celebrate their success. But you did live up to your other promise of learning your lines and being at every rehearsal. That deserves some kind of pat on the back. I'd like to see you face the kids in person and let them decide whether or not you'll be welcome at the party. Would you be willing to do that?*

Philip: *I don't really want to, but if it means that much to you, I'll do it for you.*

Ms. J: *No, Philip, I don't need you to do it for me. I want you to do it for them and for you.*

Philip didn't show up the following day. The principal called me in to say that Philip was apprehended in the act of trying to burn down his parents' house. He was taken to juvenile hall pending his court appearance. Some kids said *We told you so, Ms. J.* Other students cried and vowed to write him letters. He was given probation with community service but didn't return to the school.

At the end of the year, his dad resigned from the city council and moved the family to another state.

NOTE: Did that teach me a lesson? Yes, never give up on a student. Never ever give up. Worse than professional acronyms are the stereotypes that students and adults so easily form. All I could do was hope that my belief in Philip's potential would make a difference at some point in his life. A word to the wise teacher: If you must visit the teachers' lounge for early morning coffee or lunch, filter all teacher conversation with the determination to be a student advocate. Your responsibility is to put the student first, no matter what. You will often not have administrative or parent or colleague support. But it doesn't matter. You, the teacher, must remain true to yourself and your calling. If that doesn't work for you, please hang up your teacher hat and find a profession that has a better fit.

Every kid is one caring adult away from being a success story.

Josh Shipp

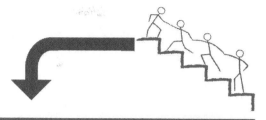

CONNECT WITH QUALITY:

EXPECT EXCELLENCE

In many classrooms across America, a popular banner or poster is tacked up on the wall that reads: *No one is a failure who keeps trying.*

Though I understand the intent, it often becomes a cop-out. All too often I hear parents and teachers say to kids, as they pat them on the back, "I know how hard you try. As long as you're trying, that's all we expect." What I believe is that *trying presupposes failure* [See Bart A. Baggett, *The Success Secrets of the Rich and Happy*]. The word *trying* is the problem. Subconsciously it's a way out, and what your mind understands is that you are planning to fail…again! If kids are told that trying is enough, they don't change anything. They are doing what they and others expect of them. If a person keeps doing the same thing over and over and keeps failing, it's because they have not changed anything.

Nothing changes unless something changes. Dennis Vicars

SCENARIO: 9th grade classroom

Ms. J: *Charlie, we need to talk. You keep missing a passing grade by the same five points. We need to see some improvement.*

Charlie: *I know, but I try so hard. I just can't seem to get there.*

Ms. J: *Charlie, let me share something with you. When you say to yourself, "I try so hard," what you are really telling your mind is that you expect to fail.*

Charlie: *But that doesn't make sense. I work really hard, but I miss the same number of questions every time.*

Ms. J: *Doesn't that consistency tell you something? Maybe you've created a habit of doing the minimum expected, and you give yourself the excuse that you work hard and try hard. To see some improvement, something has to change. Are you willing to change the way you think about that?*

Charlie: *Yes, but what am I supposed to do?*

Ms. J: *Let's talk about your study habits and your real attitude. In other words, how do you approach the situation? Where do you study? How important is achieving? What would happen if you started making 80% or above on all your work? Are you afraid of change? Are you afraid of the responsibility that goes along with being a successful student?*

Charlie: *My mom says that a "C" average is good enough as long as I try.*

Ms. J: *Is that good enough for you, Charlie? Is that what you really want? I'm going to tell you something I want you to consider: Trying presupposes failure. Do you know what presupposes means? It means you are mapping out a course for yourself to follow. This may surprise you, but more people are afraid of success than failure. If you plan consciously or subconsciously to get a "C," that is exactly what you are going to get. Is that your goal, or would you like to see what it feels like to succeed at a higher-grade level?*

Charlie: *I'm supposed to say yes, aren't I?*

Ms. J: *No, Charlie, you're supposed to look inside yourself and define what your own goals are. What does "being a C student" mean?*

Charlie: *It means I'm average.*

Ms. J: *Well, yes, a "C" grade is considered average. A synonym for average might be mediocrity. Do you want to be mediocre? Let me clarify that for you.*

[Ms. J writes vertically on the board.]

A

B

———————

C

———————

D

F

Ms. J: *If you look at a vertical scale of A being at the top and F being at the bottom, C is in the middle. Correct?*

Charlie: *Yes.*

Ms. J: *If I draw a line above the C, and you fall into that* **lower category,** *that means you are the* **Best of the Worst** *group. Right?* [Ms. J draws a horizontal line above the C grade.]

Charlie: *Yes.*

Ms. J: *If I draw a line below the C grade and now you fall into the* **higher category,** *that means you're the* **Worst of the Best** *group.* [Ms. J draws a horizontal line below the C grade.] *Think about it, Charlie. Is that your goal: To be the worst of the best group* or *the best of the worst group?*

Charlie: *Well, I never thought about it like that before.*

Ms. J: *What do you want to do about it?*

Charlie: *Get out of the "C" group.*

Ms. J: *To do that, you are going to have to set a new goal. You are going to have to change your thinking. You are going to have to quit trying and start doing. There is a big difference. Set a goal and decide a strategy to get there. Have you ever played* the game Battleship *or some other game where you had to design a strategy to win?*

Charlie: *Yeh, sure.*

Ms. J: *That's what you have to do to succeed as a student, Charlie. Trying won't get you there. You have to have a goal and a plan. I want you to go home and write down your goal for each of the subjects where you want to see improvement. Then write down three strategies that you know you can accomplish to get to that goal. Bring it to me tomorrow, and let's go over it. Are you willing to do that?*

Charlie: *Okay, I'll try...uh...er...I mean, I'll do it. I'll do it tonight. Thanks. See you tomorrow.*

NOTE: This dialogue can take place with individual students or entire classrooms. Will all students buy into it? Maybe, maybe not. It helps if you share the conversation with the parents and ask them to reinforce it. **Remember: If one student in each class changes their thinking, you are making progress. If more students change, hurray for you and for them. But whatever the outcome, quit praising them for mediocrity. Teach them a smart way to set goals, make a plan, and *get 'er done.*** [See **Odds & Ends** for *Goal Setting.*]

———— • ————

The great danger for most of us isn't that our aim is too high and we miss it, but that it is too low and we reach it.

Michelangelo

CONNECT THROUGH HIGH EXPECTATIONS:
MODEL QUALITY WORK

G iven that the vast majority of kids *can learn*, the task falls to the teacher for *inspiring* students to find their own *motivation to learn*. I am a disciple of William Glasser, the teacher-philosopher who maintains that what students want is achieving success through *Quality* work. From him, I learned to believe in a "J" curve rather than a "bell" curve. [See **Odds & Ends** for *J-Curve*.]

Students who don't know how to achieve quality work often slow their own progress or fail because they fear producing less than perfection. The teacher's job is to first show the student that quality work is achievable; second, that the teacher is there to fully support striving for quality; and third, that failure is a stepping stone, not a roadblock.

At our first faculty meeting before school starting, our administrator showed us a video about Glasser Quality Schools. Wow! Here was something that grabbed my attention. I studied the Glasser method thoroughly and applied it in a junior high classroom to great success. With the approval of the administrator, and because he knew I would put in the work needed, I required that all students get no less than 80% to pass. That took some convincing for parents and students.

The first year of using it, I had nine inclusion students out of 130 students total. Helping students understand the importance of quality work took great consistency on my part. I also spent an abundance of time outside of school hours supporting students in their endeavors to produce quality work, especially for those nine inclusion students.

A colleague of mine told me that the Glasser method is fantastic, but it doesn't work.

"Of course, it works," I said. "My students proved it. Every student by the end of the semester received no less than 80 percent on all assignments. And, no, I did not water down any assignments for the inclusion kids. They all succeeded."

"The problem," he explained, "is that *it can work*, but it's so much work for the teacher that it cannot be sustained."

I had to think long and hard about that one because I was putting in long hours to support the students who needed extra time. But I was not working smart. The second year of using the Glasser method, I wised up and learned to rely on volunteers who were a godsend. *It can be done. Your choice.*

The point is, and it bears repeating, that students want, deep down, to produce quality work. My first step is encouraging them to want to succeed. Failure is a very comfortable rut for many.

I asked the students who were used to getting mediocre grades, "What would happen if you started showing what you really can do in school? What would change?"

The answers varied: (1) My mom and dad would start expecting me to get good grades in everything; (2) I don't want that kind of responsibility; (3) No one would buy my excuses; (4) I don't know; (5) I'm afraid my friends might not like me anymore; (6) I don't want to be called a know-it-all, a geek, a nerd.

You get the idea. Deciding to be successful can sometimes cause more social than academic pressure. Once students have been bitten by the success bug, there's no going back. They are proud of themselves; their self-esteem heightens dramatically; they are willing to go out on a limb and try new things; a whole new world opens up for them. Now I ask you, "What teacher would want to hold a student back from being successful?"

———————◆———————

Someone has to raise the bar, and that person is the teacher.
Rafe Esquith

All kids can read.
All kids can learn to believe in their inherent abilities.
All kids can succeed.

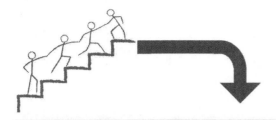

CONNECT THROUGH PARENT INVOLVEMENT:
WIN WITH DISCIPLINE

Just as I was putting things away after a long evening of parent conferences, Dottie, a new teacher in the building, walked into my 9th grade classroom.

"Hey, Dottie, how did your evening go?" I could tell she was a bit discouraged, so I sat down at a desk and pointed for her to do the same.

"I don't want to whine or take your time. It's late."

"No problem. Tell me how it went this evening."

Dottie pulled up a desk to face mine. "Well, maybe good and bad; I got a lot of papers graded." She laughed. "Only a few parents showed up even though they all seemed to agree to the time slots. And the few who did come seemed timid. It was hard to get a discussion going. It wasn't that way when I taught in elementary school."

"This is your first year of teaching secondary, right?"

"Yes, but I don't get why there seems to be a different attitude."

"I know what you mean, Dottie. I had a friend whose subject for his master's thesis was parent involvement in elementary, middle, and high school.

The results he found were right in line with what you're saying. Involvement falls off by about thirty percent from elementary to middle school, and then thirty percent more in high school."

"Isn't that backward? It seems to me that as students get older, they need more support than ever."

"I totally agree with you. There are probably several reasons for the statistics. Maybe both parents are working, especially as their children get older. Some parents feel they are not as needed; they don't know how to be involved once they are no longer baking cupcakes for classroom birthdays or bake sales. And it's awkward for some if they're divorced and don't want to show up together. I have sensed that parents are somehow rather intimidated by harder curriculum once their kids reach middle school or junior high. I've even had parents tell me that in high school, their kids are old enough to be independent. I agree with you, Dottie, it does seem backward."

"Is there anything we can do about it? I mean, my evening is a lot easier when I'm just sitting grading papers waiting for the next parents to show up, but it's disappointing, especially when the ones I really need to talk to don't bother to come. I was really looking forward to talking with Cynthia's parents. She's such a smart girl but spends most of her energy being a smart-aleck."

"Have you tried calling her parents?"

Dottie paused. "I thought parent conferences are when we're supposed to connect with the parents. They all got the letters and appointment times."

"What I've found is that most parents need a personal connection, especially in the upper grades. Most of the time when I call parents and ask them to get involved, they jump at the chance. Tell them exactly what you need and how they can help. Do you mind if I share an interesting story?"

"Please do. I'll take all the help I can get." Dottie kicked off her shoes, sat back, and sighed deeply. "I'm just beginning to realize how overwhelming 9th grade can be."

"This is one of my favorite experiences. I'm happy to share it with you and hope it helps. Danny was a pill in my seventh grade Language Arts class. Totally non-cooperative. He was smart. A good reader to the point of being a show-off, answering every question without waiting to be called on, and making fun of students with lesser abilities. He and I had been through several one-on-one discussions as well as calling a meeting with Danny's dad, his other teachers, and the principal. Every teacher had the same complaint. The dad was aggressive and defensive for Danny, saying Danny just wasn't being challenged enough. The principal told us afterward to back off; that we were just creating poor public relations.

"That afternoon I decided to call Danny's mom, hopefully before the dad got home. To my delight, her response was, 'What would you like me to do?' I said, 'Come to class and sit with him and make him do his work.' It was a leap, let me tell you. I couldn't even believe I was saying that. But you know what? She said she liked the idea."

Dottie looked perplexed. "Wasn't that embarrassing for Danny? I've heard you say *to never ever humiliate a child.*"

"You're right, but I saw this more as a consequence than humiliation. Fine line, I guess. I'm not always sure I'm doing the right thing, but I have pretty good instincts. And, yes, Danny was absolutely mortified when his mom showed up.

"Cane in hand, she came right up to me as students were coming into class and said, 'Here I am. Tell me what to do.' She saw me eyeing the cane and laughed, 'Don't worry. It's not a weapon. I have MS; I need this to steady myself.'

"Connecting the dots, I wondered how the worry of MS was affecting Danny. An aggressive father, a mother with a challenging health problem. I decided to have that discussion with her after I got to know her a bit better.

"I placed a chair beside Danny's desk and introduced his mom as a guest. The other students looked shocked, sat silently, and watched as she smiled and said quietly to Danny, 'Open your book. Get out your pencil and paper. Pay attention.' She kept him on task. All the while I worked hard to keep the smile off my face and act like it was the norm. Red-faced Danny did exactly as his mother told him.

"But that wasn't the best part. I was showing art slides to the class that went along with a novel we'd been discussing. One of the students asked how the artist made certain strokes in the painting. I didn't know and said so.

"Danny's mom spoke up and said, 'I happen to be an artist. I can bring my materials tomorrow and show the class if you'd like.'

"The next day she did just that. The students gathered around and were fascinated as she demonstrated how to make broad strokes with a pallet knife. Then she let them try it. I watched as Danny, at first very self-conscious, stood back from the group.

"When the bell rang for lunch, the students bombarded Danny with, 'Gee, Danny, your mom is so cool. You're so lucky. I wish my mom could paint.' Danny's body language slowly changed from resentment and embarrassment to pride.

"The serendipity for me was that Danny's mom then volunteered to assist me in whatever way I needed. She cataloged books for our classroom library, did laminating, made costumes for a classroom play, and sometimes sat with students helping them with their work. In fact, she became our classroom *mom,* and that is exactly what all the kids began calling her. Danny's relationship with his mom strengthened, and he began taking pride in his school work. Never again in that classroom did I have a difficult disciplinary situation. Fortunately, the word spread, and I was inundated with parent phone calls volunteering to help out when needed."

Dottie had tears running down her cheeks. I handed her a box of tissues. "What a wonderful story," she said, shaking her head. "I just don't know if I can handle it like you do."

I reached across the table and squeezed her hand. "Dottie, I've watched you with students. You put your whole heart into your teaching. Give yourself some time and trust your instincts. And remember that I'm here for you whenever you need me. Now, go home to your sweet little dog, put your feet up, and know that for today you have done enough."

Sometimes teachers are afraid to ask for parent involvement; to ask for assistance; to build relationships that permit the students to grow with a sense of pride and responsibility. Secondary teachers need to take a lesson from elementary teachers in inviting the parents to be part of the educational team. That's the responsibility of the teacher. The responsibility of the parent is to respond positively. How else are we going to make the educational process work on behalf of the student?

NOTE: I used to think I had to do everything. Then I found out how wonderfully parents can help if we allow them to be part of the team. [See **Odds & Ends** for suggestions at *Parent Conferences.]*

And then there's the Unruly Parent: Respond to the parent's need rather than reacting to your own feelings. Lead with your heart as well as your head. Plan ahead and rehearse your strategy in case this ever happens. Stay calm.

SCENARIO 1: It's 3:15 pm. Ms. J has been on her feet all day. The students, teachers, and administration were all cranky. It must be a full moon. Standing at her desk, she sorts student papers to take home to grade. Suddenly, a parent–red-faced and obviously angry–bursts through the door.

Parent: *What the h-ll do you think you're doing? I work all day and have an extra job at night just to put food on the table. Now my kid comes home telling me he needs help with his senior project.* He points his finger at Ms. J, voice level escalating. *What are they paying you for? You're the teacher. You're supposed to help him.*

Ms. J has two choices at this point. One, she can tell him to calm down and take his complaint to the office. She's not in the mood to be yelled at...**but**...she takes a deep breath, sits down in a student desk, looks up at him, and says, *I'm sorry. I can see you're upset. What would you like me to do?*

He continues his tirade. *You bet I'm upset. I don't have time for this nonsense.*

Ms. J: *I'm sorry. I didn't catch your name? Mine is Ms. J. Would you like to have a seat so you can tell me how you'd like me to fix this, um, problem?*

Parent: *I know who you are. I hear all about you from Eddie. He thinks you walk on water. Well, I'm here to tell you that just because you have a fancy degree doesn't mean you can push parents around.*

Ms. J: *Oh, you're Eddie's dad. I'm so glad to meet you. Yes, he's chosen to do a project that is related to your line of work. He speaks so highly of you.*

He casts his eyes downward and pauses. Ms. J takes this opportunity.

Ms. J: *It's Mr. Jameson, right? Please, have a seat, and we'll work this out together.*

He lowers his voice for the first time. *I'm sorry. I've had a rough day. I try to help my kid, but I just don't have much time. He kind of sprung this on me at a bad time.*

Ms. J: *That's okay, Mr. Jameson. I understand. Let's work on a plan so that we can both help your son.*

NOTE: Parents usually have a legitimate reason for being upset. If you choose to take it personally, the problem will only escalate. Take a deep breath, put yourself in the parent's shoes, and see if you can decompress the situation. Ninety percent of the time, responding with compassion and assertive listening skills will reveal that what caused the situation in the first place had little or nothing to do with you.

However, in the remote possibility that the parent storms into your classroom and does not calm down, and if you feel threatened in any way, go to the phone and call for security or administrative backup. Move toward the door so that you are not blocked inside the classroom and can flee, if necessary, to a colleague's classroom. If all else fails, scream. Always have a backup plan.

SCENARIO 2: It's 8:55 pm. Ms. J is at home, finally, leaning back in her recliner, shoes kicked off, focused on the climax of her favorite weekly television show.

The phone rings. Her spouse answers it in the other room. *Hon, it's for you. Sounds like a parent is pretty upset.* Ms. J groans. *Tell them I'll call 'em back.... Oh, never mind. I'm coming.* She gets up, cursing under her breath. *Can't I ever just have an hour to myself?!*

Hello, this is Ms. J. How can I help you?

An agitated female voice answers, *Sarah has always gotten A's on her compositions. You don't know the first thing about teaching writing. Sarah's going for scholarships. She's the best student you'll ever have. You gave her a C on this paper, and I am very angry about that. If she doesn't get a scholarship, it's going to be on your head.*

If statistics are correct that over fifty percent of communication is body language, Ms. J knows she doesn't have that advantage over the phone. She consciously decides to pour all she can muster into her tone of voice.

Ms. J: *Oh, hello, Mrs. Tate. Sarah told me you might be calling. I'm so glad you did. You know, I'd love to discuss that grade with you. I'm sure you have good reason to think the grade should be better. As a matter of fact, I was a bit disappointed in the paper myself. Do you have time to come in after school tomorrow so we can look at it together?*

Parent: *Well, I don't know. You mean you'd be willing to change the grade?*

Ms. J: *What I'd like to do first of all is see if I made a mistake in the grading. And second, I'd like to hear your evaluation of Sarah's writing. Would you be able to come to the school? Or if you'd prefer, I can meet you at the coffee shop around the corner from the school. Does that work for you?*

Parent: *Okay, well, I guess I could do that. I prefer the coffee shop, but I couldn't be there until shortly after four.*

Ms. J: *That will be fine. I'll see you at the coffee shop as soon as you can get there.*

When Ms. J goes over the organization, voice, style, and mechanics of Sarah's paper with her mom, Mrs. Tate realizes how much work the paper still needs.

Ms. J: *Sarah is a good writer, but this reads like a rough draft. I'd like to see her put more effort in to show what she's really capable of.*

Mrs. Tate: *I'm sorry. Sarah has so much going on in her life. I think she cut some corners with this one. Would you be willing to let her have time for a rewrite?*

Ms. J: *If you think that's the best for Sarah, yes, I'll do that this time. I would, however, like for Sarah to learn that she needs to meet deadlines.*

Mrs. Tate sits up, back straight, purses her lips, and replies: *You're absolutely right. I think I may have spoiled her a bit. She's had a bit of a 'princess' attitude lately, and I'm partly responsible for that. I apologize for placing the blame on you. You've taken extra time and caring, and I appreciate that. Let the grade stand. Sarah is just going to have to kick it up a notch or two.*

NOTE: First of all, when a parent calls that late, don't feel compelled to take the call. You have a guilt-free right to your privacy and your time in the evening. Your choice. If you take the call, first take a deep breath, decide not to take the situation personally, and work toward a solution rather than justifying your position or getting into a debate. Give the parent credit for having a reason for their position. Also, sometimes meeting outside the classroom is less intimidating to the parent. Pull the parent in as a team member. After all, the main focus is what is best for the student. You don't have to give in to a parent's wishes, but you can show that you are willing to compromise. Balancing between holding high your standards, being fair to all your students, and showing compassion is sometimes a bit tricky. Listen to that little "teacher voice" and go with your gut.

SCENARIO 3: The phone rings. You answer. The voice on the other end lets out a string of expletives and name-calling directed at you. Only one response is appropriate. When the caller stops to take a breath, you respond.

"I'm going to hang up now. I will not tolerate verbal abuse. If you'd like to make an appointment, please call the school office. Goodbye." [Click.]

If the phone rings immediately after, do not answer it. Having a caller-ID is a good idea. Train your spouse or significant other to check before answering when you don't want to be disturbed. Report the incident, in writing via email, to your administrator first thing in the morning. Let the administrator handle the situation.

A fine line often exists between feeling abused and working toward disarming the situation. As you practice, you'll get better at it. Having said that, most situations can be disarmed. You work hard, you care about your students, you give it your all. The hard part is not taking it personally. Being a conscientious teacher is a tall order.

———————◆———————

Sometimes you have to take the high road, even if you are the only one on it.

Anonymous

CONNECT WITH PEOPLE WHO CAN AND WILL:
THINK OUTSIDE THE BOX

Several weeks into my first teaching job in public school, the principal walked into my classroom.

Principal: *Why don't you ever ask for anything? I'm bombarded every day with faculty asking for money or time for things. You never ask for anything.*

Ms. J: *I guess I didn't realize I could. I'm used to raising money for what I need.*

Principal: *Let me give you some advice: Always ask for the moon. You'll at least get a star.*

Works most of the time! But it isn't always your administrator who saves the day.

SCENARIO: A different school, several years later. Fifth grade. Geography. The world map on the wall was the size of a placemat. No exaggeration! I wanted my students to know their world, and this was not sufficient.

Ms. J: *I need a large world map and a globe.*

Administrator: *I don't remember geography being in the 5th grade curriculum. Fifth grade is social studies. And maps and globes are not in the budget.*

Ms. J: *How do you teach social studies without knowing where in the world...?*

Admin: *Well, see what you can do. I have no money to give you. I'm late for a meeting.*

[See chapter on Administrators] Of the exceptional, the ordinary, and the challenging, I'll let you decide which applies.

Ms. J, talking to herself: *I need to take a different route. Of course, check the Internet. Aha...a 6 ft x 5 ft wall map of the world in living color. Beautiful. Only $150. The students could walk right up to it, immerse themselves in it, study it, touch it. And look at this beauty–a large interactive globe that when hooked to the computer, a student can point to any country and learn everything about it, even the language. Another $150. Hmm. How to get what I need.... Idea, present it to the PTSA. A couple of parents of students in my class happen to be officers. An in! How can I make this appeal reach their hearts and pocketbooks? Yes, use Evan, my 5th grader computer expert.*

Ms. J: *Hey, Evan, how would you like to put together a presentation using the computer?*

Evan: *Sounds fun. What kind of presentation? Do you mean in front of the class?*

Ms. J: *No, I mean in front of the parents at the next PTSA meeting. You'd have to be willing to come in the evening. Could you do that?*

Evan: *Sure, my mom always goes to those meetings anyway. I can come in during lunch if you want to show me what you want.*

Ms. J: *Terrific. See you then.*

Fast-forward to PTSA meeting. The principal reluctantly added me to the agenda.

Ms. J: *I'd like to introduce Evan. He has a presentation to show you.*

Amazing 10-year-old Evan, dressed in shirt and tie, had come early to set up the computer, white screen, and sound system. He proceeded to show the adult group the map Ms. J wanted, how to use it, and what it cost. Then he showed a 3-D presentation of the interactive globe. Wow! That's all it took. The parents immediately voted to provide the funds for both the map and interactive globe.

Ms. J: *Thank you, Evan! I never could have pulled it off by myself.*

Evan's Mom: *Thank you for the opportunity to let Evan shine. He loves doing things like this.*

Ask, and ye shall receive! The students were enthralled with the map and globe. Both became motivation to get their work done so they could explore the world. The result was several months of students choosing states, countries, islands, etc. for classroom presentations. Ms. J gave the students a list of required elements; they were free to expand on the items. The presentations were amazing. Ms. J learned more about the world from those 5th graders than she ever learned as a student herself. And no papers to grade! Just the joy of listening and learning for everyone.

NOTE: Each time I watch *Jeopardy*, I know my students are watching and could win the big bucks in the geography category. I hope they apply for College Jeopardy.

———— ◆ ————

Eventually everything connects—people, ideas, objects.
The quality of the connections is the key to quality per se.
Charles Eames

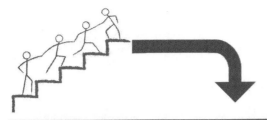

CONNECT THROUGH RESOURCES:
DO YOUR RESEARCH

Thirteen-year-old Willy seemed to be getting more difficult to handle. Each day students ran in from the playground complaining of Willy striking out at them. I was increasingly concerned, not only for the safety of other students but for Willy himself. He was of normal height for his age but had a very slight build, pale, nose too big for his face, sallow complexion, deep-set shadowed eyes, large bony hands. Willy seemed to get sick quite often.

I had used every tactic I knew. Willy tried hard at his school work, and I often saw flashes of genius on good days. But he was so easily distracted, he seldom finished his work. His thought pattern seemed to be interrupted by what his parents described as hallucinations from the prescribed Ritalin for ADHD. Constantly jerking his head, he complained of seeing shadows coming up behind him. His parents literally were wringing their hands every time we talked, not knowing where to turn for answers. The final straw happened on a Friday afternoon.

Part of the students' responsibilities was to help clean the classroom at the end of each week. Willy had signed up for vacuuming; he loved machines. Just as I turned around, he had the extended metal pipe, complete with heavy foot, raised over Patty's head. I must have leaped ten feet across the room, just in time to push Patty out of the way. The blow just missed my head and crashed onto my foot. Willy's face turned white with shock as he watched me jumping on one foot, howling with pain. Whether he was afraid of what he had done or afraid of the consequences, I couldn't tell.

Willy stammered, "I didn't mean to. I didn't mean to." Tears streamed down his face. He sat down at a desk, put his head in his arms, and sobbed. Having observed his radical behavior for some time, I had no doubt that the attack was not premeditated. It was just another of his incidents that seemed to happen spontaneously—another incident that let me know we could not continue on the same course.

When his parents arrived to pick him up, I explained what happened. They were distressed but not surprised and thanked me for having done all I could. The next day they voluntarily withdrew Willy from school rather than face consequences from the school board. My heart ached for them.

That weekend I began searching for answers. Without the luxury of the Internet to do research, I went to the local university library and started accessing medical journals to look for articles involving studies done with very bright children who exhibited radical behavior. After several hours, I ran across an article about food allergies that fairly accurately described Willy's behavior. Excited, I photocopied the article, drove home, and called Willy's parents.

"Have you ever had Willy tested for allergies?" They responded that they had him tested for normal allergies to environmental substances—ragweed, dust, pollen, etc. He seemed to always have a runny nose and colds no matter what time of year. His pediatrician had put him on antibiotics several times for what appeared to be sinus infections, but it hadn't seemed to do much good.

I spoke cautiously. "Have you ever had Willy tested for *food* allergies?" They seemed surprised and said they hadn't. "Would you be willing to?" I persisted.

I was sure they would do anything to find answers. Having given up the dream of having their own biological children, they were in their late thirties when they adopted Willy and his twin sister Wendy as infants. Wendy was the model child—sweet, well-behaved, and a good student. The contrast only highlighted Willy's difficulties. It also led the parents and doctors to believe that the problem was not genetic. Yes, they were willing to try anything.

Willy's parents found a doctor in the nearest large city who specialized in testing children for food allergies related to behavior. A week later on a Saturday morning, Willy's mother called, and in an excited voice said, "You won't believe what we found out. It's just amazing. Willy has an allergy to tomato products. The strangest thing is that he has always drowned his food in ketchup; it's his favorite thing. He's really mad that the doctor is taking it away from him. But you know what? We haven't let him have anything with tomatoes for three days, and he's already calmed down. The doctor also took him off Ritalin. Our home has been so pleasant lately. We can't thank you enough."

I was astounded. Who would have thought…something so simple as *no ketchup*?

His mother continued, "Can Willy come back to school next week if he keeps improving?"

After the school board reviewed the medical documentation, and with several days observing Willy, he was admitted back into school. Willy quietly entered the classroom, sat down, opened a book and started reading silently. I wondered if this unusually compliant behavior would last, and it did. At recess time, Willy hung back while the other students ran noisily out the door.

"Did I do okay this morning, Ms. J? Did I do better?"

I had to choke back the tears as I gave Willy a quick hug. "Willy, you were more than just better. You were a model student this morning. How would you like to be the noontime monitor today?"

I thought he would jump at the chance, but in his young wisdom, he replied, "Gee, thanks. But I think I'd just as soon be like one of the other kids, for a while at least. I think they need to find out I'm okay, not just for today, but forever, if that's okay with you."

Willy continued his good behavior, and consequently his grades improved rapidly. The other students soon accepted that what had previously occurred was not his fault, and their trust in him quickly improved. Another interesting result was Willy's unleashed sense of humor. If punning is truly the highest form of humor, Willy's intellectual capacity was exposed through his ability, every chance he got, to elicit a roll of my eyes and an audible groan from his classmates.

Willy: *Ms. J, I was just wondering why people in Asia don't like kids?*

Ms. J: *Of course they like kids, Willy. What gave you the idea they don't?*

Willy: *Well, you know, I've heard people talking about how they don't believe in euthanasia. Get it, get it?*

Willy grinned, leaned back in his chair, and basked in the limelight of his newfound fame.

Whenever a student misbehaves, you can bet there is a reason for it, and almost always, you can bet it is something beyond the student's initial control. Teaching requires understanding that and compensating with compassion and tactics. Finding the reason and a solution through research takes an inordinate amount of time and is worth the effort in the vast majority of situations.

———————— ◆ ————————

Apply the habit of going the extra mile by rendering more service and better service than you are now being paid for.

Napoleon Hill

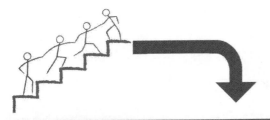

CONNECT WITH BULLIED STUDENTS:

ENOUGH IS ENOUGH!

Definition: **bully**—verb—*Use superior strength or influence to intimidate someone, typically to force them to do what one wants.*

Bullying has been around for centuries. It happens with kids; it happens with adults. Most of us have experienced it when in school, in the workplace, with peers of any age. What can be done about it?

First of all, don't kid yourself. Bullying happens in private as well as public schools. In fact, the worst bullying I have encountered was while teaching in a parochial school.

SCENARIO 1: 8th grader Julie approached Ms. J right before school.

Julie: *Ms. J, I just saw Brian and Donnie taking lunch money away from one of the 6th grade girls. She looked really scared.*

When Ms. J spoke to the principal about it—

Principal: *I'll look into it, but you know these things happen. It's just a rite of passage. No harm done.*

Ms. J knew nothing would be done because the principal was a golfing buddy with the fathers of both bullies. She called the parents of the 6th grader and told them to make other arrangements for lunch money, and in the meantime, she would keep an eye on the boys before school. Not a satisfactory conclusion, but without administrative support, it was all the teacher could do at the time.

SCENARIO 2: Public high school. Lunchtime. Ms. J walked down the long hallway toward the faculty restroom. Just as she turned the corner, she saw 11th grader Zach punch 9th grader Jerome in the stomach. Jerome doubled over with an excruciating look of pain. When Zach spotted Ms. J, he started laughing and put his arm around Jerome.

Zach: *We're just playing, right, Jerome, buddy?* Jerome, a pained expression on his face, shook his head up and down.

Ms. J looked up at Zach towering over her. *Playing or not, you're both coming with me to the office.*

Jerome wiped the tears from his eyes, pleading, *Aw, Ms. J, I'm okay. He didn't mean to hit me that hard. We were just horsing around.*

Ms. J: *Sorry, guys, I'm not buying it. This isn't the first time I've heard about you roughing up kids, Zach. It's called bullying, and it has to stop. Come with me right now.*

That they followed Ms. J to the office was a wonder, but since she knew who they were, they could hardly bolt and run. They all walked into the vice principal's office.

Ms. J: *We have a bullying situation here that I need to report.*

Mr. VP scowled: *Can it wait? I'm on my way to lunch.*

Ms. J: *I was on my way to lunch, too, but this is important.*

Ms. J explained what she had seen. She almost lost her composure when the VP responded: *You know, boys will be boys. I don't think we need to make a big deal out of this. Right, guys?*

Both boys shook their heads in agreement. Ms. J was livid.

Ms. J: *Either you fill out the report, or I will, and I will be calling the parents of both boys. Do you want to handle this or shall I?*

The VP handed Ms. J the papers to fill out, brushed past her, and went on to lunch.

Ms. J excused the boys, filled out the papers, put a copy in the principal's box, made copies for the parents, and kept a copy for her files. After school, Ms. J was called into the principal's office and put on notice that she needed to be more discreet in handling these situations or she would be written up for insubordination.

Just a couple of months before the incident, the entire faculty had been required to go through two full days of training in how to discern bullying behavior, how to intervene, and the teachers' responsibilities to report it accurately. Ms. J knew the VP had been at the training sessions. She couldn't believe her ears when he said, "Boys will be boys." That phrase was exactly what the trainer had said was no longer to be used to excuse bullying behavior. After that, Ms. J kept her eyes open for bullying situations, continued to report them, and hoped she would be supported by parents and the school board if necessary. She didn't know which was worse—Zach bullying Jerome or the VP and principal bullying her.

NOTE: You, the teacher, have a responsibility to watch for bullying, turn in the bullying situation to the administration, and fill out the proper paperwork identifying the bully and explaining what you have seen. That is your obligation.

Sometimes bullying is plain to see; other times it is very subtle. Statistically, boys are prone to physical bullying; that's easier to spot. Girls often use psychological intimidation, especially with cyberbullying. Tune in to conversations to catch that.

SCENARIO 3: Students walked into Ms. J's 10th grade English class, turned in their journals as they entered, and took their seats. They were a polite group of students. At the end of the day, Ms. J sat at her desk reading their weekly journal pages. Most wrote about something they had experienced during the week at home or school, books they were currently reading, and movies they'd seen recently. The assignment was to learn to communicate in real language rather than shortened versions they were all used to in texting. Even emailing had fallen by the wayside for most.

When Ms. J opened Tonya's journal, she was taken aback at a drawing in red of a girl hanging by her neck from a tree in what looked like a park. She was shocked by the gruesome drawing. Below the drawing was a poem revealing Tonya's distress at being bullied online by a group of 10th grade girls in her classes. The poem was printed off a computer in all bold, red font, all capital letters. The poem is much too graphic and confidential to include here.

What Ms. J did do was share the poem with the administrator who had a daughter the same age as Tonya. The principal immediately called the parents who were totally unaware of the situation at home. She then arranged a meeting with both parents and Tonya, as well as the school psychologist who took charge of the matter. When Tonya expressed being upset with Ms. J for bringing the problem out in the open, Ms. J reminded her that she had discussed with classes the need for confidentiality in journaling *except where safety was concerned.*

Gratitude to supportive administrators. The girls were banned from social media for a while. They were hopefully made to understand the seriousness of cyberbullying and the role they played in what might have been a tragic suicide. Tonya spent the next year in counseling.

Bullying happens in the hallways, on the playground, in the bathrooms, in the classroom, and on social media. Be aware. Watch for it. Talk to your students about it. Explain their responsibilities as outlined in the student handbook as well as their responsibility in their treatment of fellow human beings. Explain the difference between petty tattling and reporting a serious situation to an adult. Explain the difference between being a so-called *innocent bystander* and taking full responsibility to report incidents, no matter how trivial they may seem. One of the reasons bullying persists is that students don't often understand that as a bystander they are perpetuating the bullying. Explain this to your students in age-appropriate terms. They'll get it! They have as much responsibility to report bullying as you do.

SCENARIO 4: Fifth-grader Sammy was big for his age. The other students who had known him since kindergarten basically ignored him. They rarely tattled; they were used to nothing being done about his behavior. On the playground, Sammy preyed upon the new student, the small student, or those physically, socially, or intellectually challenged. Whether or not he was desperately lonely or just a born bully, who knew? In the classroom, he was a master at creating havoc when the teacher was busy helping another student. A bid for attention? Maybe. He was mild as a lamb when Ms. J worked one-on-one with him. Manipulation? Maybe. His dad was in prison; his mother had just been released. Both had been incarcerated for drug dealing. Ms. J's heart ached for the kid, but she knew she had to keep an eye on him.

One day Allen came to Ms. J and whispered, *Sammy has a knife. I saw it. Please don't let him know I told you.*

Ms. J waited until recess. *Hey, Sammy, hold up a minute. We need to chat.* The other students ran merrily on to the playground. *Before we go to recess, I need for you to hand me your knife.*

Sammy put his hands on his hips. *Who's the snitch? I'll bet it was Noah. He's such a baby.*

Ms. J: *That's beside the point. Please hand me the knife. You know the rules, and you know I have to report this.*

Sammy hung his head and kicked at the gravel. Then he handed Ms. J the knife—a one-inch blade—the kind that folds out of a Swiss army knife.

Sammy: *Do I get to have it back? My grandpa gave it to me. I use it for fishing. He* looked up at me with pleading puppy dog eyes.

Ms. J: *We'll see what the principal says. In the meantime, don't ever bring any kind of knife to school. Understand?*

Sammy: *Yeh, sure. Can I go play now?*

Ms. J watched as he ran over to the field, grabbed the soccer ball from Jesse who was small for his age, then proceeded to take over the game.

When Ms. J reported the incident, the principal said the knife was too small to be considered a weapon, called Sammy in for a lecture, and returned the knife to him.

Ms. J filled out a report and put it in his folder.

Two weeks later, Bonnie approached Ms. J on the playground. *Sammy has a knife. He was showing off and threatening some of the girls with it.*

Ms. J called Sammy over. *Sammy, what are you trying to prove? Do we have to go through this again? Hand me the knife.*

Sammy took the knife from his pocket and, with a blank but steady stare, handed it to Ms. J. Then he ran off to play. Once again, Ms. J turned the knife—a bit larger this time—into the office and filled out the paperwork. She also put a note in the principal's box asking for a conference with the school psychologist. The principal said she could handle this herself, and that Sammy was just probably wanting attention. She returned the knife to him after school.

You've probably guessed by now that this was not the end of the story. On the last day of school, the students and teachers stood out on the sidewalks saying their farewells.

Ms. J turned around just in time to see Sammy come up behind Jennifer, twist her arm behind her, and hold a switchblade to her throat. This time it was a very large knife.

Sammy looked directly at Ms. J: *What are you gonna do now, Teach? Suspend me?*

Jennifer stood as still as a statue, eyes wide with fear. The other students, not knowing what to do, just stared at Ms. J. Her mind raced.

Ms. J: You've made your point, Sammy. But you don't want to hurt Jennifer; she's the one who has always been nice to you. Why not pick on someone your own size? Like me. I'd like for you to hand me the knife...or I'll take Jennifer's place, and you can hold the blade to my neck. Is that what you want, Sammy? To take down your teacher? I'm a bit bigger than you are, but you're the one with the knife.

Ms. J slowly inched her way forward. By then they had attracted the attention of others. Fortunately, the P.E. teacher quietly came up behind Sammy, grabbed his forearm and took the knife away from him.

To the surprise of all the students, Sammy started crying like a baby. The P.E. teacher marched him to the office. What a way to end the school year.

Ms. J explained to the students that Sammy probably would not be bothering them any longer, gave hugs all around, and wished them a happy summer. Several parents called Ms. J the next day; she did her best to dispel rumors and calm their nerves. She also met with the principal who once again said, *I'll take care of this. You don't need to worry about it.* Nevertheless, Ms. J filled out a report and placed it in Sammy's file. Since she was relocating to another district, she never heard the outcome. What motivated Sammy to be a bully--sociopath, psychopath, or just a kid with no parenting, a kid who desperately wanted attention?

SCENARIO 5: I personally experienced bullying when I was in the 6th grade as the only white girl in a Hispanic school. Having been reared in a family with no prejudice of any kind, I did not understand why the students hated me—spitting at me and calling me "gringo," chasing me and throwing rocks at me. Why didn't the teacher, who happened to be white, step in to protect me? Why did the Hispanic principal taunt me, calling me *the little white rich girl?*

As an adult, I reflect and understand somewhat. My parents owned a motel in a downtown area of a large city. That put me in the district where most of the Hispanic service people worked. My ponytail ribbon matched my skirt and blouse, and I wore nice shoes. I was white. My dad held down a regular job, and my mom worked late into the night running the motel. After a couple of months of mistreatment, my mother asked the school board permission for me to attend a different elementary where I would fit in better. They agreed only if there was room and luckily there was.

That was a long time ago—back in the late 50s and early 60s when racial tensions ran high. I naively thought things had changed. But recently I became aware of a friend's nephew being the only white boy in an all Hispanic school. Same situation. Bullied by students as well as teachers. His parents moved him to a private school. Though he is of very slight build, he is now bullied because his parents are overweight. I frequently hear *Kids can be so cruel.* Are they naturally that way? Or do they learn from role models? A long-debated question.

However, in a school setting, most situations can be avoided if people are paying attention. I often observe teachers and/or other adults on the playground, cafeteria, bus or hall duty. They sometimes are so engrossed in their conversations with a student or adult that they are not aware of what is happening around them. And, for whatever reason, if they are aware, they fit the description of a *bystander.* This can lead to a dangerous situation. An assigned duty is just that: *A duty.* Pay attention to how kids are interacting. When body language or facial expressions seem suspicious, step in and ask questions. Decide the seriousness of the situation and whether it needs further investigation. *Always err on the side of caution.*

NOTE: You are responsible for knowing your school's policy and protocol regarding bullying and cyberbullying. See more information at *www.stopbullying.gov* as well as your state and national education websites.

———◆———

If we are to stop bullying in schools, we have to start with teachers and administrators. If we want to stop it, we have to stop it.

Chris Crutcher

CONNECT OUTSIDE THE BOX:
TAKE ADVANTAGE OF UNUSUAL OPPORTUNITIES

Ms. J is assigned to teach in a high school situation of extremely unruly students. The previous teacher quit mid-October. The students are used to running the show. Immediate conflict.

Day 1. Ms. J walks into a classroom of noisy students hanging out.

Ms. J, to a very muscular young man leaning back in his chair: *Please get your feet off the table.*

Young man, smirking: *I'll put my feet wherever I want. We run this classroom. You'll learn to adjust.*

Ms. J: *Nevertheless, we don't mistreat the furniture in this room. Get your feet off the table and mind your manners.*

Young man, getting angry: *Just what are you gonna do about it, b_tch?*

Ms. J walks over to the phone and calls security. *Please send someone to Room 210 to remove a student from class.* She hangs up and says to the young man: *Gather your books and jacket. You won't be with us for the rest of the day. I'll see you tomorrow. Bring respect with you.*

Without waxing eloquent, let's just say *things get better by March*. Ms. J is persistent, consistent, compassionate, and puts into effect the **Be Courteous** rule. [*See* chapter **Connect Through Dialogue**.] Ms. J has a reputation for being able to outlast any student reluctant to follow the rules.

During spring break, Ms. J learns about a large sailing ship that gives short trips as a learning experience about sailing, ocean environment, ecology, and teamwork. For a rather reasonable fee, they allow teachers to bring students aboard for a day outing.

Ms. J, thinks to herself: *Hmm, just what my challenging vagabonds need.*

Returning from spring break, students chat about the fun, or boredom, they experienced.

Ms. J brings them to attention: *Has anyone here been on a sailing ship? A ship with really big sails?*

The students look at her as if, *Say what?*

Ms. J: *Would you like to go sailing?*

The students sit up with eager looks.

Ms. J: *All we have to do is get permission from your parents, raise a bit of money, and find transportation to the city dock.*

Long story short, they do just that…except for finding transportation. A few of the students have cars. They agree to share gas money. Ms. J doesn't ask about insurance. She doesn't ask anything. She drives her own car. [I cannot advise going out on a limb like this. It wouldn't be professional of me. Caution is wise.]

Ms. J's favorite holdout, Trevor, goes along, complaining all the way. Once on the ship, the broad-grinning, muscled Captain takes over. Ms. J watches in awe as he sizes up the vagabonds. He then gives each student a duty.

Captain: *Before we start with the chores for the day,* [Students' mouths fly open at the word "chores."] *we're going to hoist the sails. Here, young lad, grab the end of this rope. You girls come and hold on here.*

Soon all the students are lined up holding onto ropes. The crew begins to sing: *Yo-o heave-ho, Yo-o heave-ho,* as they pull on the ropes. The students have no choice but to pull or get knocked down.

Captain: *Come on, you landlubbers, let's hear you sing out.*

Timidly at first, then gradually with more vigor, the students sing robustly. Winds catch in the sails, and the ship begins to move. The excitement is electric.

Captain: *Come over here, lad. What's your name?*

Trevor.

Captain: *Well, Trevor, how would you like to be First Mate today? Take a seat at the wheel.*

Trevor stands in shock, his mouth hanging open.

Captain: *Well, don't just stand there, Mate. We're headed out to open sea, and someone has to steer this ship. Sit here. Now put your hands on the wheel like this. You don't have to move it much...not until I tell you to go left or right. If you're good at it, I'll let you turn it around when we're ready. And from the looks of you, I'd say you're just right for the job.*

Trevor, eyes wide, grins, and sits with his back board-straight. The Captain puts a real sailor's hat on Trevor's head. Trevor gives the hat a tug. Ms. J stands with tears in her eyes, wondering how the Captain chose this particular student, the student who most needed the attention, the student who had resisted her at every turn. Serendipity!

The day goes smoothly. By lunchtime, the crew knows each student's name, pulls them into tasks that the students genuinely seem to enjoy, teaches them about sea creatures as they pull up buckets full of small thrashing octopi, squirming fish, and beautiful starfish. Ms. J watches in awe. Vagabonds metamorphose into dutiful, obedient, happy kids.

Under the watchful eye of the Captain, Trevor has by now learned how to handle the wheel to keep the sails full. At the end of the voyage, Trevor does indeed get to turn the ship back toward the dock. It isn't an easy task. At the dock, one of the crew explains that they hire 11th and 12th grade students to be part of the crew during the summer. The Captain hands out applications to those interested. Ms. J sees excited looks on the faces of several students. The day ends with the students and crew posing for a photo in front of *their ship*. A photo for each of the students is sent to the school within the week. Ms. J still has hers proudly framed on her office wall.

Ms. J enters a different classroom the next morning. The vagabonds are transformed into mild-mannered, excited students who stand taller, laugh easier, and look, well, *gentle*. The rest of the year is a joy.

NOTE: I've never regretted taking that chance. One of the senior girls, Ruby, sailed on the ship that summer and saved enough money to go to the local community college. She had been pregnant that first semester and now was the sole supporter of her baby boy. Ruby was cream that rose to the top. I'll never forget the look on her face as she reached for her diploma at graduation. As for *Captain Trevor*, he came back the following year to apologize for giving me such a hard time. I have no doubt that he is successful in whatever he has chosen to be as an adult.

A good teacher has been defined as one who makes
himself progressively unnecessary.
Thomas J. Carruthers

CONNECT BY GOING THE EXTRA MILE:

JOURNEY ON THE HIGH ROAD

Ms. J walks down the hallway, picking up bits of trash, a nickel, two dimes, and a penny. *How is it that kids walk past money without bothering to pick it up?* She had collected over twelve dollars the past year in change picked up in the hallway. *Walking past litter is bad enough, but kids ignoring money that was just lying there? Go figure!*

Just as Ms. J passes the girls' restroom, she hears stifled sobs. Peeking in, she sees eighth-grade Katy sitting in the corner, knees hunched up to her chest, tears streaming down her face.

Ms. J: *Katy, Katy, what in the world is the matter? Why are you so upset?*

Katy: *Ms. J, they ruined it. They hate me.*

Ms. J grabs a wad of toilet paper from the first stall and hands it to her. Katy wipes her runny nose while uncontrollable hiccupping sobs erupt from deep inside. Ms. J slides down the wall, sitting beside her, and puts her arm around Katy's shoulder.

Ms. J: *Tell me, Katy. What was ruined? And who hates you?*

Katy: *They all hate me. Someone took my social studies project—my big poster I worked so hard on—I worked for days and days on it—and now it's gone. They took it. They all hate me.*

Ms. J: *Let's start from the beginning. Maybe the poster got misplaced. I'll help you look for it.*

Katy: *No, I looked everywhere. And then I asked the custodian, and he went through the trash, and even the dumpster, and he found it. He found it all torn and crumpled in the dumpster! My project. I worked so hard. And I was so proud of it. And the deadline is tomorrow, and I won't be able to enter it into the contest for the social studies fair. They all hate me. They've hated me from the start.*

Ms. J pats Katy's shoulder, gets up to get more tissue, and wonders what to do next. What could she say to this sweet young girl? The other girls were insanely jealous of Katy. The boys who couldn't have her for a girlfriend taunted her. She was too pretty, too smart, too well dressed, too well-mannered. She had it all. Blonde hair, almond brown eyes, brains, a beautiful singing voice, an infectious laugh, and a quick wit. She was the envy of all. Ironic that they had elected her class president and then turned against her. Ms. J can't find a reason except for the fickleness of teenagers. She has observed Katy's kindness, her lack of self-absorption, her willingness to do whatever it took to complete the task at hand without seeking any recognition. She had given her all and gotten nothing but hurt in return--one of those lifelong teenage scars.

Ms. J: *Katy, may I tell you something? I know nothing will erase this hurt, but there is a way to conquer the problem.*

Katy: *Thanks, Ms. J, but there's nothing you can do. I'm sorry. I don't mean to feel sorry for myself. I'm just upset. I'll be okay.*

Ms. J: *I know you'll be okay because you always pull yourself together and make it work. I've been aware for some time about how things are going, and I know you've been the target of some of the kids. But you know, sometimes kids don't know the difference between admiration and envy. I think they voted you in as president of the class because they admire you, and because they know they can count on you to do a good job. At the same time, they envy you. And rightly so.*

Ms. J gives her a gentle squeeze and continues. *If you let me, I'd like to show you a way to come out on top in this situation. Will you allow me to do that?*

Katy: *I guess so. I don't mean to take your time. What should I do?*

Ms. J: *The big project is due tomorrow, right?*

Katy: *Yes, but it took me days to get the first one done. There isn't time left. And I don't want to ask Mr. Mac for more time because then the kids will think I'm his pet, and he told us before that no exceptions would be made. I just can't get it done in time.*

Ms. J: *Katy, I know you want your project to be the very best it can be. And, no, there isn't time to do it by yourself. But I think we can get it done together. Let's start right after school, and I'll help you. Under the circumstances, I think that would be acceptable. You do the brainwork, and I'll do whatever you tell me to. That way it will be your creation. We'll just reconstruct your original project.*

Katy: *Wow, Ms. J, you'd do that for me? It might take all night. I mean, it's going to take hours.*

Ms. J: *That's okay. Sometimes an all-nighter can be a lot of fun. I'll meet you in my room right after school. Is it a deal?*

Katy brightens up, smiles her perfect-teeth smile, and dries her eyes. *Thank you, Ms. J, thank you so much. I feel so much better now.*

After school, Katy busies herself watering the classroom plants until the last student has left.

Ms. J: *Okay, Katy, let's go. I called your mom and explained the situation. She's picking up poster board and meeting us at your house. She invited me for dinner, so we're going to get this project done, no matter how long it takes.*

Katy: *I'm so excited. This is going to be fun!*

Ms. J: *Just one thing, Katy. You must promise never to say anything to anyone about this, except your parents, of course. I've talked to the custodian, and he knows our secret. He's very angry with the culprits but has promised not to say anything to anyone. Got it?*

Katy: *Got it, Ms. J. Cross my heart.*

Ms. J, arriving at Katy's house: *Hi, Mrs. Perkins. Thanks for offering your help.*

Mrs. Perkins: *Well, of course. I have to say, I am very unhappy with whoever did this, and Katy's dad is steaming. He's planning on getting to the bottom of this. What they did is just vicious. Katy poured her heart and soul into that project, and she's done nothing to deserve this.*

Ms. J: *I know exactly how you and your husband feel. But when he gets home, I'd like for Katy to be able to explain to you both about how she wants to handle this. In the meantime, we'll get started.*

Mrs. Perkins clears the flowers off the dining room table to make room for them to work. Katy lays out the poster board, pens, and the materials gathered from the classroom—maps, books, magazines, and an old history textbook full of sepia-toned photographs.

A couple of hours later, Katy's dad enters the living room. Katy is busy reconstructing her original idea with a few revisions. *Hey, that's looking good. It's really kind of you to come help her, Ms. J. Um, could you step into the hallway for a moment?*

Ms. J: *Of course. I'll be right back, Katy.*

Mr. Perkins: *I'm going down there in the morning and have a talk with the principal. This is harassment, and I won't stand for it.*

Ms. J: *I do understand how you feel. I've given this a lot of thought because I truly believe a bullying situation needs to be addressed straight on. However, I know these particular kids very well; I know their parents. I don't think this is the usual case of bullying. Harassment, maybe, but I think it's because, well, because Katy shines in everything she does with a truly humble spirit. Some of the students are very envious and don't know how to separate their admiration of Katy from their envy of her. I'd like you to give Katy a chance to explain her rationale. You can take it from there.*

Mr. Perkins: *Well, alright. I'll see what she has to say. But if this doesn't turn out well, I'll follow through.*

Ms. J: *Agreed.*

Just then Mrs. Perkins calls them all to dinner. She apologizes for eating in the kitchen, but Katy has obviously taken over the entire dining and living room with her project. Over dinner, Ms. J urges Katy to explain their strategy.

Katy: *Mom and Dad, I know you're upset, and believe me, I was plenty upset, too. But we've decided to do what Ms. J suggested, and that's what she called "taking the high road." We're not going to do anything about this—nothing. And I don't want either one of you to say anything to anybody.*

Mr. Perkins raises his eyebrows. *But, Katy, this isn't right. If we don't nail those mean little culprits, they'll just do it again.*

Katy: *Dad, that's a chance I'm willing to take. But if Ms. J is right, it won't happen again. It's sort of like, how did you say that, Ms. J—catching more flies with honey than vinegar?* Katy looked at her parents, pleadingly. *Dad, please, just go along with me on this. You understand, don't you, Mom?*

Mrs. Perkins: *Well, yes, I think I do, and it just may work. I think it's a great plan.* She looks at her husband. *I know how you can get. But Katy needs to do this her own way. Let her fight her own battles and let's stay out of it this time.*

Mr. Perkins harrumphs a bit but finally agrees. Katy's mom clears the table, her dad goes into the living room to read the evening paper, and Katy and Ms. J get back to work. A couple of hours later, Mrs. Perkins brings in a cake and glasses of ginger ale. Both stand up to stretch, enjoy the treat, and wish Katy's parents goodnight. They still have a great deal of work ahead of them with Katy giving direction, and Ms. J following along.

At 5:30 the next morning, Katy's mom comes down the stairs to make coffee just as Katy is cleaning up the scraps of paper, putting away the markers, and rubbing her dry, tired eyes. Katy's mom looks at the display—a three-dimensional design, enhanced by Katy's determination to make this project even better than the last one. Mrs. Perkins smiles as she hands Ms. J a cup of coffee and gives Katy a sweet squeeze. *That's my girl. I'm really proud of you.*

Katy slips the poster into its plastic sleeve and looks at her mom with a shy grin, *"I'm really tired, Mom. Could I have a cup of coffee, just this once?"*

Mrs. Perkins: *Not on your life, Kiddo. Get upstairs and take a nice long shower. End with cold water, and that will wake you up. Now get going so you're not late. Thanks, Ms. J, we owe you one. You've gone above and beyond.*

Ms. J: *You don't owe me anything. Believe me, when I see the looks on the other kids' faces, I will know who the culprits are, and it will be worth every sleepless moment. I'll let you know how it goes. Thanks for your hospitality. I've got to run along home and get ready. I'll call you later with all the details.*

Ten minutes before the tardy bell, Katy pokes her head into the classroom. *Ms. J, may I leave the poster in here for safe-keeping until social studies class third period?*

Ms. J: *Go across the hall and see the secretary, Katy. I told her you'd be storing it in the office. I don't want any of the kids to get any ideas. I've arranged for a class-cover, so I'll be in Mr. Mac's room for your presentation. Just don't let on, okay?*

Katy: *Good idea. See you later.*

Just before third period, Ms. J walks into Mr. Mac's classroom. *Hey, Mr. Mac. I hear you're judging the poster contest today. Dave is covering my class; okay if I hang around and see how the kids have done?*

Mr. Mac: *Sure. Glad to have you. Want to help me judge?*

Ms. J: *No, that's okay. I've been hearing about this project for weeks and just want to see what the kids came up with.*

The students, many bleary-eyed and carrying last-minute posters, file into class. Just as the tardy bell rings, Katy walks in with her poster. Scanning the room for reaction, Ms. J sees the jaws drop of two of the boys huddled together with one of the girls. Their eyes meet each other's with a look of surprise and disbelief. Katy leans her poster facing against the wall with the others while the three seeming culprits whisper to each other. Ms. J stands at the back of the room. Katy glances at her, both suppressing looks of delightful collusion.

Mr. Mac tells the kids to take a seat and bring each poster up in turn for individual presentations. Many of the posters, true to Mr. Mac's high standards, are creative, artful, and excellent in content. Some, however, seem thrown together without much thought or care. Katy stands up for her turn and picks up her poster. Ms. J watches the three culprits as Katy turns the poster toward the class. An audible gasp sounds from the three-presumed guilty, but Ms. J merely glances in their direction. With great composure, Katy gives an articulate presentation, then smiles at Mr. Mac and takes her seat. The students clap politely.

Several minutes after school ends for the day, Katy bursts into Ms. J's empty classroom and shuts the door. She literally jumps up and down, laughing gleefully. *Ms. J, we did it. We did it! Thank you, thank you, thank you.* She gives Ms. J a quick hug and continues, *...and you know the best part? Kevin and Shawn and Trudy were all whispering after class, and then Janie came and told me she heard them say they didn't know how I turned in a poster like that. I know who did it. I'm sure it was them.*

Ms. J: *Okay, Katy, but remember our agreement. You chose to take the high road. You may get some satisfaction out of knowing who the culprits are, but our revenge was in your successfully completing the poster, right? Did Mr. Mac judge them yet?*

Katy: *No, he said he'd let us know tomorrow, but you know what? I don't even care if I get first or second or third or anything. I just feel good that they didn't keep me from getting the assignment done. I feel good that we, well, that we overcame their nasty trick.*

Ms. J: *Good for you, Katy, and that was the point, wasn't it? That is the sweetest revenge. It's our secret, Katy. And I'm going to make a wager that those three are going to do all they can to become your best friends. You mark my words.*

Just then the custodian pokes his head around the corner. *Hey, Katy, how did it go today?*

Katy: *Just great, Mr. Jarvis, Just great.* He gives Katy a grin and a thumbs-up. She knows her secret is safe with him.

———— ◆ ————

People find meaning and redemption in the most unusual human connections.

Khaled Hosseini

CONNECT WITH THE MOST IMPORTANT PERSONS:

THE CUSTODIAN AND SUPPORT STAFF

Okay, so maybe *most-important person* is a bit of a stretch. But if you've been teaching for more than three years, and you haven't yet made friends with the school custodian(s), get a clue. Your life will be so much easier if you appreciate what they do to keep the school running smoothly. You do your job; they do theirs; treat them as part of your team.

Custodians have their own agenda for keeping the school in good shape. Most have limitations on time as to what they are able to do inside classrooms; that varies by school. Find out what they are expected to do for you, and what is not their responsibility. The nicer you and the students keep the classroom, the more the custodians are going to appreciate you and be willing to go the extra mile for you when needed.

Some examples:

I need an additional whiteboard. The principal tells me to go on Craigslist to see if I can find one that I can afford. Really? I speak to the custodian who tells me there's an extra one in the storage facility. The next morning, the whiteboard has been installed.

I have a closet in my room that needs shelves. I don't ask the principal this time. I ask the custodian. Without doing a work order, within the week she has the shop class make and install shelves.

My responsibility is to make sure the whiteboards and dust tray are cleaned every day. The custodian tells me she'll do it for me; that I just need to write "Save" on those items I don't want to be erased. She tells me she's doing this for me because my room is always neat and clean.

Having read the research on fluorescent lighting causing stress, dental problems, and discipline issues, [Google it!] I learn that full-spectrum lighting diminishes those problems and is available for installing in the same lighting system. I approach the principal to see if he will let me do my own research by installing full-spectrum tubes. He lets me know that's not going to happen unless I pay for it myself. I enlist the help of a few parents, purchase the lighting, and ask the custodian to install them. "Just for you," he says, "but don't tell anyone else." I grin. By the way, the atmosphere in the classroom changed. I could see students visibly taking deep breaths and relaxing. I don't know if it helped their teeth.

SCENARIO 1: The first day at a new school, I go directly to the custodian's office. Yes, the small, dank little room with the wet mop smell. I reach out my hand and introduce myself. *Hi, Joe.* I've made a point to find out his name ahead of time. I sincerely say. *I'm Ms. J, the new English teacher. I'm just curious. What's your favorite snack, Joe?*

He looks at me with a knowing smile; he can tell I'm a seasoned teacher. *It's brownies with walnuts. And don't bother to bake them yourself. I like the ones at the supermarket right down the street. That will do just fine.*

NOTE: The next time I need a custodial favor, I leave the brownies with a note written on nice stationery on Joe's desk. I'll be at the top of his list of priorities, and my classroom will be the cleanest in the building. I remember not to cross that fine line between sincere appreciation and manipulation.

SCENARIO 2: When a student accidentally threw open the classroom door too hard, bashing a hole in the wall, I left Joe a request for repair. Schools usually have a protocol that involves writing out a work order, getting it approved by the administration, and waiting an interminable time for repair. However, because of my good relationship with Joe, the repair was made that afternoon, and all was well. The next morning, I left a very special card on Joe's desk, thanking him for his immediate response and beautiful craftsmanship.

Joe stepped into my classroom the next morning before classes began. I wondered if something bad had happened because Joe had tears in his eyes. He held the card in his hand. *Ms. J, in 22 years of working in this building, this is the first time I've ever gotten a thank-you card. I can't tell you how much this means to me.*

NOTE: Small efforts can have large impacts. Remember to say *thank you* and keep it relative to the job completed. Joe went out of his way for me; the time and effort it took to say a special thank-you was well worth it. Custodians are part of your team; remember to treat them as such.

Children and teachers deserve a clean, orderly place in which to learn, socialize, and work. Parents as taxpayers and/or tuition payers deserve good stewardship of expensive school buildings and grounds. Whose responsibility is it?

SCENARIO 3: Seventh-grade class, the third week of school.

Ms. J: *Guess what, my sweet cherubs. Today we're going to take responsibility for those desks you're sitting in. I want each of you to close your eyes, place your hands under the tops of your desks, and tell me what you are touching.*

Hands go under the desks and are immediately jerked back with cries of *yuck, eeuew, yech, what is that?*

Ms. J: *That yucky substance is the thoughtless act of someone chewing gum and, rather than taking the responsibility of wrapping it in a piece of paper and throwing it properly in the trash, sticking it underneath your desk. Can you imagine someone committing such a vile and nasty act?*

Ms. J then hands out plastic spoons—the short, inexpensive kind—not the elegant plastic less-easily-broken kind. *I want everyone to stand up, turn your desks over, and begin scraping. In the unlikely event that your desk happens to have no chewing gum, look around for the ugliest desk and help your neighbor.*

Steven: *Hey, I ain't gonna do this. That's the janitor's job.*

Ms. J: *Is that right? Do you really think cleaning up after a thoughtless renegade is in the custodian's job description? I don't think so. Your parents' taxpayer money goes for better things than scraping off chewing gum.*

Brian: *Yeh, and you're supposed to be teaching us; not making us clean up after other kids. I didn't do this, and you can't make me clean it off.*

Ms. J: *Yes, you're right. I can't make you, and I won't. But why do you think we have a "no gum chewing" rule here at school? I will ignore that rule in this classroom if you will all participate in giving us a clean slate to begin with and keep it that way. Let's take a vote. How many agree to clean up and keep it cleaned up so that you can chew gum responsibly? [Count...] Good. I thought you'd make an intelligent decision. Now, let's get it done, and hopefully you will appreciate what the custodian's real job is here at this school next time you're tempted to dispose improperly of chewing gum or any other trash.*

NOTE: The reason for the plastic spoons is that when the plastic breaks, the students can hardly avoid touching the gum. It's gross so pass around the antibacterial lotion when finished. The exercise takes only about ten minutes and usually solves the problem once and for all.

The "no gum chewing" rule is usually the longest-discussed item on the agenda at the first faculty meeting every year in every school. Some issues are easily resolved if we communicate with students and learn to negotiate with them reasonably.

Be a good role model. Never walk by trash or a piece of paper lying on the floor of the classroom or in the hallway without picking it up. This is excellent modeling for students. And, by the way, if you think the trash might be a note from one student to another—the way it's folded is a dead give-away—put it in your pocket or in the drawer of your desk and do not read it until the students have left the room. See chapter on *Passing Notes*.

SCENARIO 4: High school class

Ms. J: Last Saturday night I had a party at my house and invited several friends. And do you know what I discovered? I have some very disgusting friends. I found candy wrappers in some of my potted plants and paper napkins thrown under the table. Can you imagine doing such things in your own home or that of your friend's house? Who do you think cleaned it up? [They point at you.] Yep, ya got that right. I cleaned it up. I know none of you would ever do anything like that in your own home or in our very own classroom, and I appreciate the pride you take in keeping our space clean. The custodians appreciate it, too. Thank you.

NOTE: The fact is you're sick and tired of picking up after the kids. But after this little speech, you've set before them the expectation, you continue to be a consistent role model, and you often praise them for being good citizens. It doesn't work with 100 percent of the students, but it works for enough of them to make everyone's life easier, including that of the custodians when they come into your room to clean every night.

SCENARIO 5: Write thank you notes with your classes, all grade levels.

Ms. J: Today we're writing thank you notes to people who rarely get any thanks, and it has to be someone other than a teacher. Look around the room, think about people in this building, and remember something that someone does to make life better for everyone. The smaller the detail, the better. Be specific. For example: Instead of saying, "Thanks for all you do," mention the specific thing that they did. We'll share some of these when you're done. [Let the students see you also writing notes and be willing to share if asked. I use colorful index cards and have stickers available for a bit of decoration on the cards.]

Susan: *Dear Mr. Jonas [custodian], Thank you for installing our new pencil sharpener. I was really getting tired of my new pencils getting chewed up.*

Eric: *Dear Mr. Jonas: Thank you for emptying our trash every day. That's my chore at home, and I'm glad I don't have to do it here at school, too.*

Angie: *Dear Mrs. Adams: Thank you for having tapioca every Wednesday in the cafeteria. It's my favorite, and my mom always burns it.*

Peter: *Dear Mr. Burns [assistant principal]: Thank you for greeting us every day when we get off the bus. My dad is always grumpy when I leave home, and you always make me feel better.*

Sonia: *Dear Ms. Grant [school secretary]: Thank you for loaning me your stapler the other day when I was putting up posters in the hallway. That was very nice of you.*

Tommy: *Dear Ms. J, [That's you, the teacher]: Thank you for making us write thank-you notes. I've never written one before, but I think I'll do it more often. It feels good. P.S. I know I wasn't supposed to write to a teacher, so I wrote another one to the janitor.*

Dear Students [You write on the board]: *Thank you for taking time to write thoughtful notes. I appreciate the specific items you have mentioned, your originality, and your sincerity of expression.*

NOTE: The repercussions are far-reaching, beyond the classroom, beyond the school year. Writing thank-you notes is becoming a lost art. Reinstate it and repeat often.

I've had discussions with other teachers who think I go overboard. Those same teachers are the ones I hear speaking to the custodian in brusque tones as if that person were a second-class citizen. I learned to not ever judge a custodian's status in life. Two cases in point: One of my beloved custodians was a retired teacher, just coming back to be with kids, be in a school, and earn some extra money. Some teachers never took the time to get to know her.

Another custodian, Bruce, made an effort to look out for the marginalized students in junior high. He was an avid reader and could often be heard discussing books with students. Students would stop by his workroom before school just to trade books and discuss some of their mutual hobbies. Come to find out, Bruce had a Master's in Science, was a bowling champion, and enjoyed fly fishing. He quit a high-paying corporate job to avoid stress and enjoyed the satisfaction he got in being the custodial shepherd of the school. Those of us who took the time to get acquainted with Bruce were very blessed in having a very good friend as well as appreciating his conscientious care of our classrooms.

SCENARIO 6: Fifth Grade Class

Josh: *Ms. J, tomorrow is my birthday. Is it okay if my mom brings in cupcakes?*

Ms. J: *Sure, Josh. Will you please remind her about allergies...chocolate, peanuts...you know the drill.*

Josh: *Yeh, I know. My mom's vegan. She's really into all that stuff, so you don't need to worry.*

Ms. J: *Terrific! Tell her to come at about 3 o'clock, and we'll make sure we have all our work done.*

Josh: *Can we play Twenty Questions?*

Ms. J: *Sure. That will be a nice way to end the day. I'll let you be in charge.*

Next day: The thirty-minute party went well. Josh had appointed his best friend Ben as his assistant. After the last round of Twenty Questions, Ben got a roll of paper towels and disinfectant spray. He went down the aisles, sprayed each desk, and handed a paper towel to each student. Josh carried around the trash can to collect the paper products. Someone had accidentally dropped icing and cake crumbles on the carpet. Josh leaned down, cleaned it up without complaining, pulled the trash bag out of the can, tied it up, and set it by the door. He then went to the board and drew a big red heart. Inside he wrote a note to the custodian: *Mr. Kane, we cleaned up the room. Take a break! You're the BEST EVER. Signed, Josh and classmates.*

On St. Patrick's Day, Mr. Kane brought in shamrock-shaped sugar cookies with each of the student's names written in green frosting. He then wrote on the board in green: *Happy St. Patrick's Day to my BEST EVER students!* They all gathered 'round for a group hug. Now that's real connecting!

All of this, though lovely to behold, did not happen automatically. I consistently role-modeled keeping a clean, organized classroom; I explicitly instructed students in my expectations as well as teaching them that having a party was a privilege. I also did my share of reminding until no longer necessary. We hit a few bumps along the way, but gradually the students came to understand the gratification in doing their part in keeping a tidy classroom. The stress taken off me was well worth the initial effort. Every situation can be a learning opportunity.

———————— ⋅ ♦ ⋅ ————————

Good habits formed at youth make all the difference.
Aristotle

CONNECT PROFESSIONALLY:

DRESS PROFESSIONALLY

I like walking into a school and knowing immediately who the principal and assistant principal are judged solely on how they are dressed. I like knowing who the teachers are and appreciate paraprofessionals who live up to that name *para*, i.e., *alongside in a supportive capacity.*

I like meeting a principal who dresses in business dress. I like the air of respect it brings to a building, to the personnel, to the profession. I like knowing that the person in charge has enough respect for themselves and for the profession to strive to be, well, professional. And I like teachers who look professional rather than as if they were going to a school picnic.

I taught for thirty-five years in private and public schools and have witnessed the gradual deteriorating of professional dress during that time. As I recall, it started with Friday Spirit Day. On Fridays, we all wore some sort of dress pants or skirt along with our school colors or school polo. We did it to show spirit. Spirit Day then became "dress-down" day. I remember teachers commenting: *When did Fridays cease to be "spirit" day and become "grunge" day?*

The effect was enormous. Fridays became *watch a movie/video day, celebration day, reward day, party day, Fun Friday.* Some students began skipping Fridays because... *We don't do anything in class anyway.* Some teachers still hold the standard high, but I'm guessing they are few and far between.

I must ask: *How much has lowering our dress standards influenced lowering our academic standards?* I think the question is viable and the answer is important. If the influence is as I imagine–fairly substantial–then I will address the question to superintendents and administrators: *What are you going to do about it?*

I'll give you a firsthand example of how dress affects students. For a few years, I taught at a parochial high school. The dress standards were fairly stiff. The students were allowed to wear jeans only on Fridays. The jeans could not be too tight, too worn, torn, or have frayed hems. But students pushed the limits, as students often do, wearing them too tight, etc. The school board then said, *No more jeans.* The students rebelled.

Okay, they said, *we'll follow the rules. Give us another chance.* The school board agreed. But after a few weeks, the students blew it—again! So, no more jeans. The school board suggested uniforms. The students and parents disagreed, saying it hampered individuality

As an extreme response, and to make a point, the Associated Student Body (ASB) got together and decided they would institute their own dress code: Dress pants and shirts for the guys, only dresses/skirts for the girls. No more jeans. The parents rebelled. "Too expensive," they said. The students pressed on, hoping to make their point and get the school board to bend.

It worked. Under parental pressure, the school board caved and said, *Okay, we're giving up having a dress code.* To the surprise of everyone, the students refused to give up their newly instituted dress code because...in their own words...*We like the way everyone acts when we are more dressed up. We are nicer to each other. We act like ladies and gentlemen. The boys treat the girls with more respect. The girls are even nicer to other girls. We don't want to give up our dress code.* The student dress code remained in effect, enforced by the students themselves.

I, for one, was very proud of the students for taking the matter into their own hands. I have not stretched the truth here; this actually happened just this way.

What about uniforms? I applaud those schools and school districts who insist on uniforms for the students. It does indeed level the playing field. From time to time, news talk-shows highlight schools and students from underprivileged as well as prep schools who have done something worthy, and these students are usually wearing uniforms—often dress pants/skirts, dress shirts, blazers, and ties. I am impressed, and they seem to have a certain pride about themselves.

Back to the issue of dress codes for teachers, paraprofessionals, and administrators. While visiting a high school, I looked around for the administrator. A man entered the lobby area. I assumed, from his dress, that he was working on the sprinkler system being installed outside the school. He wore a plaid shirt that was wrinkled, khaki pants with frayed hems, and scuffed shoes. To my surprise, when I asked to see the principal, it was indeed this same man. And it wasn't even dress-down Friday. I thought, *Well, it must be just an off day; maybe he had some sort of special circumstance.* But, no, I've been back several times since, and he's dressed the same. I have also seen him in action in the hallways and classroom. He gives little respect to students and teachers, and they return little respect. Would it help if he dressed professionally? I don't know. Would it be worthwhile to find out? Absolutely!

SCENARIO: I walked into a 9th grade classroom. A tall, middle-aged man, dressed in blue jeans and a polo shirt, was walking across the tops of the student desks. He jumped down and introduced himself as the assistant principal. Students were lying about the room, texting, listening to iPods, playing games. It was the middle of the classroom period; it was not on a Friday. I'm sure my eyebrows raised, and my mouth fell open. I got the impression that the assistant principal was trying to relate to the kids—that he was trying to *be cool.* After he left the room, the students made fun of him, saying unkind and disrespectful things about him. Would his being dressed professionally and acting in a professional manner have changed all that? Maybe, maybe not. But how much has lowering dress standards contributed to a general lack of respect for education in general?

The next question is: Whose responsibility is it? Does a dress code need to be enforced from the top down? [Pun intended.] Why would that be necessary for administrators, teachers, and paraprofessionals who call themselves *professionals*? Why are we not capable and responsible enough to think this through and do it for ourselves? What does *being a professional* include?

I taught for many years in various buildings in a district where most of the staff, from the administrators to the custodians, dressed professionally. The schools had a professional air about them that you could feel from the moment you walked in. The teachers and paraprofessionals interacted with respect for one another. Not everyone necessarily liked each other or agreed with each other, but they treated each other with professional regard. No dress code existed; it was just understood that we all, in our various academic professions, wanted to look the part.

Education is not what it used to be, academically or otherwise. Our nation's schools are in trouble. Yes, I know there are those isolated schools and programs that are making great gains through innovation, technology, raising standards, making school practical, producing soaring test scores. But that isn't the norm. Where do we begin to "fix" this problem? Will enforcing dress codes across America solve the problem? Probably not. Will raising the professional standards for administrators, teachers, and paraprofessionals at least have some sort of positive impact? I think so. Whose responsibility is it to promote change? Who will step up to the plate to save the day? Where do we go from here?

———◆———

Few places are more important for dressing appropriately than the workplace,
where a professional appearance is crucial.

Susan C. Young

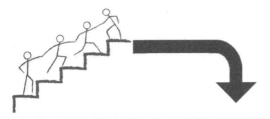

CONNECT WITH ADMINISTRATORS:
THE TEACHER'S RESPONSIBILITY

This chapter is for teachers, but I hope administrators and parents will read it as well. In every profession, the players need to learn how to *play the game*, whether it's the ability to negotiate, be discreet, bite your tongue, step back and wait, move out on that limb, be politically correct, or just understand the politics of the situation.

What I want teachers to understand is that being a principal is like being caught between a rock and a hard place much of the time. The principal is the middle person—between faculty/parents/students and school board or superintendent. They need to please both sides as often as possible, or their job is on the line.

I've worked with a wide spectrum of administrators. The ones I admire are those administrators who are willing to stick their necks out in difficult situations. What I don't admire is those who become administrators because they know they'll have better pay as well as a better pension in the end. The education profession is a high calling. The decision to be an educator should be based on a passion for helping young people prepare for a bright future. Pure and simple. If that's not the reason to be in education, other professions might be more suitable.

Now, the **exceptional**, the **norm**, and the **challenging**. I'm not trying to be insulting or unfair. I just want to be honest. Let's begin with the worst so we can finish on a high note. I've varied personal pronouns. The "he" or "she" is alternated but does not imply good or bad for either gender. These descriptions are based on personal experiences.

The challenging administrators–Beware!

▶ He dresses unprofessionally and yells at students and teachers. The tension in the building is depressing. Classrooms are in disarray. Chaos reigns. The turnover in teachers escalates every year. Parents are unhappy. Teachers are unhappy. Students show no respect.

▶ This is her first time as principal; hired without the benefit of first being a vice principal. She had a good reputation as a classroom teacher but has no natural instincts for being an administrator. She wants to be a "friend" to the students, caters to only the elite of parents, dresses like a floozy, humiliates teachers in meetings, is wishy-washy with discipline, does not understand the importance of safety rules. Everyone is unhappy except her because she seems oblivious to all that matters to everyone else.

▶ The principal calls an emergency morning faculty meeting before school starts. She is wringing her hands; tears spill down her cheeks. She announces a student suicide. The faculty is in shock. In sobs, she tells the sad story, then throws up her hands and says, "I just can't deal with this. You'll have to handle your students the best you can. I'm taking leave for the day." She exits the room. The faculty is angry but relieved she'll be out of the building because they have found she doesn't do well in an emergency. It is up to them.

NOTE: Many teachers are afraid to speak out for fear of retaliation. That's a legitimate fear in many cases. First, try being diplomatic; talk with an administrator about the situation. If that doesn't work, talk with experienced colleagues who are in leadership positions. *A word of caution about insubordination.* For your own sake, learn where the lines are that you should not cross. Though life should be fair, and you want to do what you can to make it that way, it doesn't always work. When you realize you are in an untenable situation, you have to make a decision. If you must stay in that school, pull back and determine to let it go instead of eating at you. If you have a strong union, document carefully the situations you find uncomfortable and garner support. If you have the opportunity to transfer to a different school or district, do that. Life is too short to be in an unhappy situation for very long. Do what is best for you, and, in the long run, it will be best for the students, too.

The normal administrators—These are generally tolerable.

- ▶ They are friendly, stand out in the front hallway during passing times, always smiling, trust the faculty to do their jobs, provide what they need when needed.
- ▶ Discipline? They support whatever teachers do but don't get involved.
- ▶ Parent involvement? Whatever parents think best.
- ▶ Creative ideas? Things teachers want to try? *Sure, go for it. Behind you 100%.*
- ▶ Problems? They are sure the teacher or student or parent can work it out.

- ▶ Need for fire/earthquake/lockdown drills? No worries; it's not going to happen here.

You get the picture. It's a happy place, but you're on your own. Work with your experienced colleagues as situations arise. If you have a strong union, get advice from them. Use diplomacy, be professional in all you say and do, and keep good records to back up your actions and decisions.

NOTE: I would like to insert here an example of a "good" administrator. Hmm, I'm trying to think of one between *okay* and *excellent*. Ah, yes, in all of my thirty-five years of teaching, *there was one*. Nice guy, supportive, kept the school running smoothly, was open to suggestions. Progressive? Not really. Willing to go beyond the budget? Not really. Beholden to the school board? Absolutely. Willing to go out on a limb? Never. A fair disciplinarian? Yes. My students and I, mostly trusting my own instincts and without interference, had a joyful, gratifying year of stimulating creative learning.

The exceptional administrator—Sorry to say, I experienced this only once, but what a joy!

- ▶ She was for several years a classroom teacher, then a vice principal, then an administrator. She studies the profession, works long hours, hires only the teachers with the best reputations.

- ▶ She genuinely connects with students, teachers, staff, and district personnel. She cares about her faculty and staff, treats them like family, knows their spouses and children's names.

- ▶ A teacher emergency? She gets someone to cover the class or does it herself.

- ► She writes grants on behalf of students, teacher retreats, updates in technology, whatever will enhance the school community. Teachers gather energy from her.

- ► She is always in her office before anyone else arrives and leaves after everyone else is gone for the day. She is often there on weekends and holidays.

- ► If a teacher is doing an excellent job, she commends them publicly. If a teacher is falling short, she confidentially helps them improve.

- ► She is a role model. She will not ask a teacher to do anything she wouldn't do herself. If a teacher wants to try something new, she discusses the pros and cons to help the plan succeed.

- ► The building is clean, organized, runs smoothly. Everything is up to par. Teachers are free to focus on student success because she is taking care of everything else.

- ► When she asks teachers to go above and beyond, she compensates them in some way for their time and expertise. *Any supervisor worth his salt would rather deal with people who attempt too much than with those who try too little.* –Lee Iacocca

- ► She is a consummate professional and expects her faculty and staff to be the same.

- ► Teachers choose to teach in her building; most stay until they tearfully retire or die.

A truly great principal is hard to find, difficult to part with, and impossible to forget.

Anon

So, how do you connect with your administration?

If you are a fairly new teacher working with an administrator who realizes you need to ease into a more-than-full-time job, you are fortunate. Regrettably, some administrators pile all the extras on a newbie just to see if they will hang in there.

Have you been assigned extra duties until the faculty feels you have paid your dues, e.g., playground duty, lunch duty, bus supervision duty, dance chaperone? Hopefully, most schools have learned to share these extra duties equally with all taking turns on a published schedule. If not, don't allow others to take unfair advantage. If needed, talk with your team leader, chair of the department, or administrator who will be evaluating you. Avoid gripe sessions with other teachers. Always follow the protocol.

If you are in one of those schools where you can *elect* to supervise an extra duty, my advice to you is "Don't." After your first three years, when you feel you have a handle on your teaching responsibilities, and you want the extra money offered for other duties, then that's your choice. The irony is that your first three years is probably when you need the supplemental income. I urge you to resist. You need before school, lunchtime, and after school for planning, grading papers, conferring with colleagues and working with students. *Be good to you.*

Now, let's get some venting out of the way. I dare you to read the following poem in one breath. On second thought, I don't want to be responsible for your keeling over, so take your time. I didn't write it to discourage you; rather, to let you know we teachers are all in the same boat. Let's learn to row together as a team.

Attention Teachers: Just One More Thing...

A new contest the principal says:
We'll read, we'll write, and see which class has the
most books and poems and stories and things
and by the way they must learn their math facts and remember to
turn in your scores so I see which teacher's kids are the

smartest and when you get that done remember to send

in your report on how much money was raised in the technology

drive and did you do your report on which transportation your

students use to get to school and home? Oh yes parent-teacher

conferences are coming up soon so get those grades

into the secretary before the weekend so that she can

print out the reports and remember to contact all the parents

and try to give them the conference slot they desire because

most of them work full time and we need to be accommodating

which reminds me that when you have class parties--birthdays and

Halloween and Valentine's and Winter Break (which we all know

is really called Christmas) and St. Patrick's Day (be careful

about Easter because of religion you know) when you have

those parties remember that a lot of students nowadays have

allergies so leave out those treats that have nuts or eggs or milk

products or flour and try not to do too much sugar and by the

way when you have recess duty and after-school supervision,

keep those playgrounds clean we've seen a lot of

trash out there remember to recycle and dump your own recycle

bins goodness knows the custodians have plenty to do and while

you're at it keep those kids out of the mud puddles and off the

ice too much mud and dirt and snow are being tracked into the

building and by the way we'll be having a fire drill later today so if

it's raining just consider it a lockdown. What you say?

You don't have a key to lock your classroom?

Well do the best you can and it's been noticed that we've been using

too much paper so your copy ID and password have been

changed and a limit will be placed on the number of copies

you can make so be careful and if you run out don't bother the

secretaries with it goodness knows they have plenty to do so

please be accommodating which reminds me I know we've asked

a lot of you this year but remember to keep up those professional portfolios because your evaluation is coming up soon which reminds me that the state tests will be scheduled for two days next week

and three days the following…or is it the other way around… we'll let you know as soon as we figure it out but get those kids ready for it because 30 percent of your evaluation is based on how those kiddos do on the test and if they don't measure up well neither do you but then that's why we pay you the big bucks and in these tough economic times we know you're just feeling lucky to even have a job even if you only get paid for 7-1/2 hours each day for 178 days and have to take work home every night and I do appreciate everyone keeping up those bulletin boards and remembering to change them every month…Well, enough said, have a nice weekend.

See you bright and early Monday morning.

--RJW

With that venting out of the way—yes, I wrote the poem—feel free to read/ rant aloud any time needed—here is some important information for you to consider.

The teacher's responsibilities to administrator(s):

No Blindsiding

Never let your administrator be blindsided by information you neglected to share. No matter how egregious the deed may seem to be, do not allow yourself to feel so intimidated that you cover it up. If anything happens inside your classroom or area where you are supervising that needs reporting, you must let the administration know immediately. If your administrator hears about the situation from a student, a parent, or another faculty or staff, the situation will escalate, and the outcome will not be in your favor. Verbally, in person, report what happened. Then follow up with a written report—a copy to the administrator and a copy in a file you keep at home. Do not keep copies that may be damaging to you, in your desk drawer or file cabinet. Protect yourself.

Evaluations

It's time for your evaluation. You're on pins and needles. You work extra hard on your lesson plans, making sure all objectives are written on the board, all materials are assembled, and the paperwork is turned in on time to the evaluating administrator. You decide what to wear—something professional but not stuffy, comfortable, cool enough since you might be a bit nervous and sweaty. You prep your students ahead of time. "Be yourselves and be on your best behavior. The administrator is here to evaluate how you are learning as much as she is to see how well I teach. Let's help each other shine."

The first thing to internalize—Do not be defensive. Know your lesson plan inside and out. Be prepared for the unexpected, whether it's a student discipline situation or a question that arises that you do not know how to answer. Be ready and willing to say, "I don't know, but we'll take time to find out."

Use eye contact with each student. Look out across your classroom in random order; do not allow your gaze to dominate to the right or left. [I was reproved for this.] Call on an equal number of boys and girls. If a student is otherwise occupied or just not paying attention, walk up to them and stand beside their desk until you get their attention

Be aware that a student or two may decide to sabotage your presentation.

Correct negative behavior by silently letting them know you are aware of the plot. Use humor to cajole the students into good behavior and appropriate responses. Avoid embarrassing any student.

SCENARIO: Nick and Laney are passing notes and snickering during Ms. J's introduction to the lesson. The evaluating administrator shifts in his seat, watches them, and makes notes. Ms. J keeps talking, walks around the room and comes up between the two students' desks.

Ms. J: *Nick and Laney, how about saving that humorous anecdote for later when you can share with the class. For now, we need your full attention. Thanks for your cooperation.*

When the administrator presents you with your evaluation, check it for accuracy. If any negatives are given, rather than be defensive, ask for clarification and suggestions for improvement. If you believe you are being targeted or criticized unnecessarily or unfairly, hold your response. You can later check with your union representative or a trusted colleague who has worked with the administration longer than you have. Follow up as necessary. Just remember that none of us is perfect, and that you need to have as open an attitude toward learning as you expect of your students.

Most of all, relax as much as possible. Focus on the evaluation as a learning experience for you and a chance to shine in front of your administrator.

Here's a tip that will help you feel more comfortable. At least once a month, invite your administrator to visit your classroom. If you are presenting your favorite lesson, students are giving presentations, or something special is happening, this is a good time to show your administrator what's happening in your classroom. If you are having some challenges, invite your administrator to observe you and give you feedback. Do this before your evaluation to give yourself time to work on weak areas. When the administrator comes in for your evaluation, your improvement will be noted.

NOTE: I once had an administrator who made daily rounds and stood out in the hallway listening through the air vent. She was well aware of happenings in all classrooms. Don't let that make you paranoid. If you're doing a good job, you'll be glad for the eavesdropping.

Parent Contacts

Teachers who regularly contact parents are appreciated by administrators. The time you take to meet with parents before or after school and to make calls on evenings or weekends will be time well spent. You will build bridges on behalf of your students as well as accomplish some good public relations for your school. *See chapter on Contacting Parents.*

Faculty Meetings

Interesting and worthwhile faculty meetings vary widely with administrators. Some are get-to-the-point and get-out-of-there. Mr. M. was like that. Our faculty meetings never lasted more than 30 minutes after school once every two weeks. Tight agenda. Discussions and questions timed. If anyone wanted to stay past the 30 minutes, Mr. M. would stay. All others were excused.

Contrast that with Ms. L's hour-long weekly breakfast meetings. Departments took turns fixing and serving hot meals. Some found it delightful; others grumbled about the time. Much humor was enjoyed, camaraderie was built, and the agenda was usually covered. The meeting ended with several names being drawn for door prizes.

Your responsibility in faculty meetings? Listen. Give your input, keeping it short and pertinent. Don't worry about someone disagreeing with your opinion. It's all opinion! Take notes. Follow up when necessary. Be a good team player.

NOTE: *Do not ever grade papers in faculty meetings or talk to your seatmate while someone is presenting.* It's disrespectful, to say the least, and sends a message to your administrator that you do not have a sincere interest in the agenda or your colleagues.

Appointments with Administrators

If you think your days are full, double that for most administrators. Rarely do they have time to get their work done during the school day. Phone calls, meetings, budgets, discipline, observations—their days are very long and most work evenings and weekends to catch up. Well, the good ones seem to.

Sometimes you have a quick question and can poke your head into the administrator's office and get a quick answer. Emergencies may arise when you need their attention immediately.

Under normal circumstances, however, when you have an issue to discuss:

- Make an appointment.
- State the issue and how much time you need, e.g., seven or twelve minutes.
- Keep track of your time during the appointment and stick to what you said.
- Have your notes ready and take notes during the meeting.
- Respect their time and expertise.
- When your time is up, stand up and thank them. If the administrator wants to prolong the meeting, that's their call. If you have an appointment and need to leave, let them know that.
- Reschedule to resume if needed. Most administrators will appreciate your professional attitude and will more readily entertain talking with you next time the need arises.

Professional Distance

Whether you like it or not, whether it's stated or not, a hierarchy exists. Accept that and respect that. Administrators usually have favorites, just like teachers do. This is resented by some. Do not let yourself be drawn into "the inner circle." You will be wise to know where the professional line exists. Even if the administrator steps over the line, be sure to stay on your side. This takes some savvy and often some experience. Hopefully, you will learn without getting burned. If you do make a mistake, do what it takes to acknowledge and rectify the error, and don't let it happen again. Maintain a professional distance.

Body Language

Whether you are in front of your class, in a committee meeting, sitting in your administrator's office, attending a faculty meeting, meeting with colleagues or parents—be aware of your body language, including your facial expression.

Practice in front of a mirror (seriously):

Lift your eyebrows slightly;

Sit a bit forward in your chair;

Unfold your arms;

Keep your hands in your lap or on the table;

Respond facially and/or verbally in a positive manner to what is being said.

For some, this will take practice. You might want to ask a colleague to observe you. We often do not realize what strange mannerisms we have. Break your bad habits so that you appear open to communication and learning.

Committee Meetings

You have a responsibility to participate in a certain number of extra activities.

You may be asked to volunteer, or you may desire to be on certain committees. Find a good balance after weighing the time required with your other obligations. Do not succumb to overextending yourself just to make a good impression on your administrator. As a member of a committee, carry your part of the load. If you have an assignment to complete, get it done on time. Build your reputation as a responsible colleague who has much to contribute. Just don't overdo it!

Lunchroom Decorum

Be careful of lunchroom gossip. Often teachers lapse into a griping session about the administration, district policies, personnel, or students. Do not indulge. Excuse yourself quietly. Walls really do have ears, and you do not want to be a part of listening to, or spreading, negative information.

Bottom Line

A school is a bit like a kitchen. *Too many chefs spoil the broth.* We all want to educate students to grow up to be leaders as well as team players. Therefore, we must practice what we teach.

———— ◆ ————

Many receive advice; only the wise profit from it.
Harper Lee

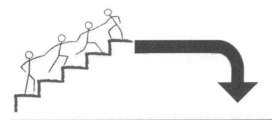

CONNECT WITH SUBSTITUTES:

MAKE THE JOB EASIER

Generally speaking, preparing for a substitute is a pain in the neck. The flip side is that being a substitute can be daunting for the sub if the teacher has not prepared adequately. Do yourself a favor. Get a handle on this for several reasons:

- Quit feeling guilty when you need to call for a sub.
- Cut down on preparation time.
- Help the sub have a good day in your classroom.
- Prepare plans that do not leave you with reams of papers to grade when you return.

HERE'S HOW:

1. Prepare a substitute folder with all information a sub will need, including emergency plans, a map of the school *with the faculty restroom highlighted*, bell schedules, phone numbers for the office, library, security, and the

name, room #, and phone # of a nearby teacher. For each class period, name a student as the teacher's helper. Choose someone shown to be responsible but not necessarily the top student in the class. Many times, you can avert a disaster if you use this opportunity to give the unlikely student a chance to shine.

Whatever you do, don't leave the sub guessing about anything.

2. Explain the heating/cooling system. Is there a thermostat in the room, an on/off button somewhere, a fan available? Can the windows be opened safely?

3. Have seating charts available. If you don't usually have assigned seating, let your students know that when a sub is present, they must accommodate the sub by sitting in assigned seats. Have a chart on the wall for that purpose so that students know where to sit when they enter. Make sure the seating chart you give the sub is *readable as the sub stands at the front* of the classroom. Think about this: Taking attendance will be quick and easy, and the sub is not left guessing how to pronounce unusual names. The sub will also be able to identify, without having to inquire, disruptive students or those students who have a special need. Provide a clipboard with a sign-out/sign-in sheet for students leaving the classroom for bathroom, office, etc. Students sign with times leaving and returning. This provides an uninterrupted flow and protects you and the substitute in case something happens.

4. Understand that many students dislike, feel insecure, and even resent having a sub. If you have to be gone more than two days, some students, especially younger ones, will feel abandoned; their compassion for your reasons for being gone is often short-lived. Prepare your students ahead of time. Talk to them about potential situations in age-appropriate terms. Tell them that when you return, you expect to get a good report from the

sub, and that they are to treat the sub with respect, helping the sub in any way they can. Explain how difficult it is for a sub to walk into a classroom cold, not knowing names, not knowing the routine, and having to learn the lesson for the day in very short order. Set the standard high. If you must use bribes, e.g., *I'll give out tootsie pops if I get a good report,* then call a bribe by its real name: *a bribe*!

5. If you're only going to be gone one day, think through your lesson plans and decide what you can give the sub to do that will be worthwhile but not daunting to the sub or to the students. Do NOT leave a video for the sub to show unless it is part of the curriculum. A video, or any kind of work that is simply *a filler*, sends a very poor message to students about the value of education. Do NOT expect your sub to grade papers, make copies, or be your secretary.

6. If you are gone for two or more days, you might want to leave a phone number where you can be reached for clarifying expectations of the sub and the students. Keep it simple as well as worthwhile for everyone concerned.

7. Be nice to your sub-clerk or person in charge of scheduling subs. That is a horrendous job! A thank-you note now and then will be much appreciated.

8. When you find a sub you like, ask for permission to call that sub directly next time. Good subs are very valuable. Let them know you appreciate what they do. The converse is that if you have a sub who does not do a good job or is unduly hard on your students, let the sub-clerk know that also. Some school districts or buildings have a "Substitute Response Report" for the sub to report on the teacher and for the teacher to report on the sub. Use it and learn what you can from it. If a sub leaves names

of disruptive students, deal with that privately when you return. *Do not ever discipline an entire class for the action of a few.* If a student feels they have been treated unfairly by the sub, tell the student to write a "My Side of the Story" paragraph and take that into consideration before meting out consequences.

Personal Benefits and Obligations of the Teacher

Know your rights. Read your contract and your faculty/district handbook. Be responsible for information that directly affects you.

Dump the guilt trip for being absent. Some of you are parents who have to use sick or personal time to take care of children ill at home, dental appointments, family emergencies, etc. Most school districts grant a certain number of days for this purpose. Use them with a clear conscience. You might want to set aside a few days for your own emergencies, but don't drag yourself to school when you feel ill just because it's too much trouble to plan for a sub. If you have that *Substitute Folder* prepared in advance, even with some "in case" lesson plans to fall back on, you will be able to call in and rest easy that all is well.

Most school districts have a maximum number of days you can accumulate. Some districts pay you for unused sick leave. Know what the plan is. I was rarely absent and over the years accumulated over 180 days of sick leave. The district policy was to pay for one-quarter of unused sick leave which I collected when I left that district. I gave them back three-quarters of a school year. Did anyone appreciate my personal, and maybe not necessary, sacrifice? Absolutely not!

Do what is good for you and for your students: If you are sick, stay home, guilt-free. If you need to make an appointment for whatever reason, use the time given you. If you are feeling stressed, a malady that often comes across as *grouchy* to your students, give yourself permission to take a *mental health day.* If only I had taken more of those.

Personal leave days are different. Check your contract to see how *personal leave* is defined. If it's unclear, check with your union representative or someone who will give you a clear, fair, and honest answer. Do you need to get your hair done and can't find any other time? Want to go skiing or fishing or hunting? Be discreet, but *personal leave is usually defined as no one else's business.*

Also, check your contract and/or faculty handbook for *bereavement days.* I've known teachers who used up all of their sick days to attend a family funeral, or to take care of family business after a death, not realizing they had bereavement time coming. Read your contract and know your faculty handbook.

———————◆———————

Teachers are not the saviors of the world, but those who are born to teach come very close. It's okay if you find out it's not for you. Decide to be the best…or find a different profession that brings you joy.

R. Janet Walraven

CONNECT WITH TEACHERS:
BE A SUCCESSFUL SUBSTITUTE

The last five years of my career, I experienced short and long-term subbing, pre-school through high school. People substitute for various reasons: to make ends meet, to make extra money for a vacation, supplement income for a sick spouse or child in college, or hope to get a foot in the door for a long-term assignment or job. My heart goes out to you. I hope this helps you not *just get through each day* but find pleasure in connecting with the students and staff. You, too, deserve joy each day.

Substitute Teaching Tips:
- Life as a substitute is so much easier if you build a reputation for being one of the best.
- Some districts have an orientation required for substitutes before the school year begins; be grateful for those. Some districts have nothing; you just go in "cold."

- Know ahead of time where the buildings are. Do a test drive; know where to park and whether you need a permit for your car. Do not leave any valuables in your car.

- Use professional business cards to introduce yourself and leave one on the teacher's desk if you wish to return.

- Dress professionally. You only get to make one first impression. Wear appropriate, comfortable shoes. If you are substituting in elementary, you might want to take an extra pair of shoes for that gravelly or muddy playground.

- Be prepared. Take a snack, lunch, water bottle, sweater for cold classrooms, a folder of creative, age-appropriate lesson plans just in case, and whatever else you personally need to be comfortable. Keep these in a handy place at home or in your car.

- The first time in a building, arrive early to orient yourself. Find the faculty restroom or one nearest your classroom(s). Ask the secretary if there is anything unusual happening, e.g., fire drill, assembly, etc.

- Go into the workroom to see if other subs have arrived. Talk to them; ask any questions you might have. Get to know them. A word of caution: Some may be eager to tell you the negatives; take what you need to know but don't let that affect your attitude. You need to start your day believing all will be well.

- Make sure you can find the lesson plans for the day. If there aren't any, don't get frustrated or critical of the teacher. Give them the benefit of the doubt for whatever reason they are absent.

- Introduce yourself to the custodian(s). They can be a great help to you.

- Look around the classroom for whatever might assist you in having a smooth day—schedules posted, temperature control, seating charts, emergency procedures, discipline procedures, etc. Get a feel for that teacher's protocol.

- Be at the door to greet students as they come in. Wear a friendly smile. Introduce yourself and let them know a bit about you and what you expect. Write your name on the board.

- When you have a break, walk down hallways and peek into other classrooms. Get to know the teachers. If the classroom feels welcoming, leave your professional substitute card to let them know you're available.

- If you enjoy a building, the staff, the students, let the secretary know you will be happy to return. If you don't enjoy the classroom, don't go back. That's the upside of subbing—you get to decide where you want to be.

- Leave a concise report for the classroom teacher(s). If difficulties arise during the day, ask yourself if it's necessary to let them know or let it go.

- Don't let one rascal steal classroom time from the other students, the majority of whom are complying with your expectations. Take the names of students who are non-cooperative and let the classroom teacher deal with consequences. If a student is out of control, call the office and have them removed from class. I received the following note from a student: *You're a really strict substitute. Thank you. I hope you come back more often.*

A WORD OF CAUTION: If you need to report something that is a safety concern for you or the students, report it to the classroom teacher, secretary, custodian, or administrator. Otherwise, keep any criticism to yourself and decide not to return to that classroom or building. I, for one, will not return to a school where the administration is not supportive; where a classroom is a mess; where students are out of control; or where I am not comfortable with the situation. Keep the criticism to yourself; they will get the unspoken message. Once you have established your reputation as one of the "good subs," you will have plenty of calls for those jobs you enjoy.

Be professional and have a positive spirit. After all, it's a day in your life, and you deserve to experience it joyfully. *Thank you for being willing to take on this challenging profession.*

———————◆———————

Individually we are one drop. Together we are an ocean.
Ryunosuke Satoro

ODDS AND ENDS

ABUSE/NEGLECT—Familiarize yourself with your district/school policy regarding the reporting of students who seem to be neglected or abused at home or elsewhere. You have a responsibility, an obligation, to report suspicion or fact—anything you see or hear—that points to a child being in danger. Be sure to document the situation in writing, giving copies to your administration and keeping a copy for yourself in a confidential, locked cabinet or safely at home. My first go-to person is always the school counselor or social worker. If you do not feel you are being taken seriously, speak confidentially with the administrator. If that doesn't work, go to the district office. Make sure you are keeping a paper trail. This can be a sticky business without proper support. Protect your students and protect yourself.

ART—Make friends with your art teacher(s). One of the most interesting high school projects I did was assign students to write a poem about their childhood. Then, unsigned, I gave those to the art teacher. She had her art students create an artistic rendering that fit the poem. Because they didn't know with whom they were working, they were all motivated to do their very best. We had an exhibition, inviting parents and the community, where both students showed their work together. If you're doing a play, ask the art department to help you with backdrops or art objects that would be useful. That way more students have a showcase for their work.

BATHROOM PASSES, K-5—Elementary schools usually have methods for least disruption. Classes line up for bathroom breaks before and after recess, lunch, and special classes like art, music, etc. An idea for individual passes: Keep a stock of small paper cups, two different colors or scenes [avoid stereotyping]; also have two larger plastic cups, one for boys, one for girls. During class time, allow only one boy/one girl to go to the bathroom at the same time. Example: Boy picks up the plastic Spider-Man cup and sets it on his desk; then takes a small red paper cup as his hall pass and goes to the bathroom. Upon returning to the class, he throws the paper cup in the recycle bin; he returns the Spider-Man cup to the designated spot. This avoids interruptions and lets the teacher know who is out of class. Paper cups thrown away after use by each person is more sanitary than everyone touching the same hall pass, especially when going into a restroom. The procedure takes a couple of days to get used to but will save time and trouble in the long run. **Note:** You are responsible for your students at all times. Any student in the hallway during classes should have a pass. Let your substitute know your procedures.

BELLS—If your building has bells to begin and end classes, do yourself a favor and ask your friendly custodian to put a piece of acoustic tile over that outlet or speaker. Teachers actually have been known to go deaf after many years of having that buzzer blast their eardrums. I actually taught at a school that didn't have bells, and it was wonderful. The class was started when the teacher stood at the front and asked for their attention or took attendance. The class ended according to the time on the clock, and the teacher said, "Dismissed." What a civil way to start and end classes! I have tried—without success--to wage a campaign to get rid of bells at every school. I'm telling you, the bells are stressful!

BIOGRAPHY FAIR—This was a tradition at our elementary school for 5th graders. Each student chose a famous person who had done something important to benefit the country or the world. Teachers coordinated so that no two students chose the same person. That took some research on the part of the students to find someone they felt connected to or admired—presidents, world leaders, Nobel Prize winners, Native American chiefs (very popular), authors, scientists, musicians, and artists. This search included much incidental learning. Students worked on the project in class for about a month but had to create their visuals (error-free) outside of school. Students wore costumes of their characters and prepared a memorized speech as if they were that person. They had to know their character well enough to answer reasonable questions. The Fair was held in the school gym—one hour for setup and changing into costumes; two hours for community members to attend. Parents and community were invited; the turnout was huge. A LOT of work for students and teachers but very gratifying for everyone involved.

BIRD WALKS—Some students are experts at taking teachers on bird walks, i.e., going off subject. Sometimes it happens innocently. Teach your students the difference between a bird walk and incidental, productive, worthwhile learning. Even with that, be brief and get back to the subject. Sidestep intentional bird walks with, "Let's save that for another time."

BIRTHDAY CALENDAR—K-12—Hang a calendar on the wall. Have those students who wish to have their birthday recognized write their name on that date. Decide how you want to celebrate students and be consistent. For those students who have birthdays that fall on holidays or during the summer, tell them to choose an alternate date. **Note:** Be sensitive to those students who have religious reasons for not celebrating birthdays.

BOOK REPORTS—No more, please! **K-12:** Do not ask students to write laborious reports. It kills the joy of reading and adds to your grading load. At most, have students make bookmarks or creative posters (extra credit) for their favorite books; pass them out to other students. If you are not a techie yourself, ask a techie student or tech guru in your building to set up an interactive system where students can chat with each other about books they are reading. *Keep alive the JOY OF READING.* How else will they become lifelong learners?

BULLETIN BOARDS—Make bulletin boards relevant to the curriculum. Don't take away from your preparation time—let students create; only display corrected work but include all students at some point. Enlist parents for decorating, especially at holiday time; change at least once per month. Choose three or four students per month to decorate a section of a bulletin board, e.g., "All About Me" to include photos of places they've been, family, hobbies, etc.

CLASSROOM DÉCOR—Don't overstimulate. Keep your classroom organized, neat, clean and relevant. Have a nice balance of color and interest. Most students focus better with less. Some bare surfaces are a relief. Less is more! **Note:** The only time I break this rule is for scavenger hunts, e.g., Route 66 memorabilia for teaching *Grapes of Wrath*; photos/articles/etc. for teaching the Holocaust or Shakespeare. Make it relevant, interesting, and temporary. Old, outdated posters that have yellowed over the years? Trash them. If you don't have a budget for aesthetics, enlist art students to help you. Make sure they've signed their work and get accolades for it. **Elementary and middle school**—Hang items from the ceiling—make it worthwhile, e.g., ghost spirals with math facts written on them; poems on hearts or shamrocks; social studies facts on landmarks that students create. Enlist tall parents for assisting; you might be surprised how many are willing to drop by before or after work. *Do not allow students, parents, or you to stand on desks or chairs to do anything. It's dangerous.*

COMPASSION—Observe the faces and body language of your students. You can often tell if something is awry. Talk to them privately. If their dog or goldfish died the night before, ask the other students to show compassion. If *your* dog or goldfish died the night before, let the students know you are sad. They want to know you are human. **Note:** Do not ever cry in front of your students to garner their sympathy. Expressing sadness verbally is fine, but boohooing is not. Students tend to feel insecure, even guilty, in a situation they don't know how to handle. Your job is to role-model strength.

COMPUTER SKILLS—Teach keyboarding skills from the get-go. First-grader Jamie spent 15 minutes per day on a computer keyboarding lesson. She finished the year at 25 wpm. Yes, fingers are big enough from first grade on. And yes, many writers and journalists use *hunt-and -peck*. That doesn't mean it's preferable or that anyone should emulate them. Work with a computer teacher. Expectations should be to require excellent keyboarding skills before asking them to do written assignments on the computer.

COURTESY CONTRACT—Various behavior contracts are available online; choose one or make up your own. Suggestion: Advise students of the following procedure--On the first day, give two copies of the contract to each student who signs both and takes both home. Parent/Guardian signs both and keeps one; student returns one to the teacher who keeps it on file *for reference when needed*. It's the students' first assignment; they bring it back the next day for an *A grade*, 2nd day a *B grade* (a good start). Students who do not return the contract by the 2nd day get a call home and a zero grade. A *C grade or less* is the road to mediocrity or failure. Don't allow students to settle for that. [See **Appendix** for example.]

CRITICAL THINKING—*The aim of education should be to teach the child to think, not what to think.* John Dewey.

Critical thinking can and should be taught from at least 3 rd grade up. One of my favorite critical thinking exercises with elementary and middle school students is to play *20 Questions*. Teach them to start broad and narrow it down. Preface each question with: *Would it help us to know…?* Example: *Would it help us to know what color it is? Would it help us to know where this is taking place?* Make a game of it to see if they can get better by guessing the answer in 15, then 10, then 5, then 2 or 3 questions. Kids are amazing; they like challenges.

Junior high and high school students need a bit more of a challenge. Pose a subject—a question. Challenge them to ask higher level thinking questions on the subject instead of thinking they have to know the answers. You might even disallow answers. Have them form everything in a question and push for higher level thinking. Lucy, Charles M. Schultz's *Peanuts* cartoon character, sits at her 5-cent psychiatrist stand and says, "If life has more questions than answers, be sure you're the one asking the questions."

Example: Use *Stories with Holes.* [Google it.] I always start out with "The man with the mask was afraid to go home." The students have to ask questions to figure out the situation. *Would it help us to know...?* Once the students get the hang of it, they become better exponentially. I often use this near the end of a class period, allowing at least fifteen minutes the first time around. If time runs out, don't give them the answer; let them stew about it overnight (or research the answer). After a few times playing the game [thinking critically], the students will be getting the answer within two or three minutes. It's exciting to watch their minds work.

ELEMENTARY NO-NO'S—Please don't cover the walls with lists of spelling words, grammar, math facts, etc. If you want to reinforce a concept, do one at a time, e.g., Noun—a person, place or thing; when accomplished, take that down and put up the next one. Less is more!

EXPLICIT DIRECTIONS—What seems clear to you may not be clear to students. In giving an assignment to write an *essay*, a student asked what that was. When I explained, she said, "But what does it stand for?" I was puzzled. She went to the board and wrote: *SA.* That's what she thought I was saying. Don't assume anything with any grade level. Assure students that you want them to ask clarifying questions.

I once made it a point to write out an assignment giving very explicit directions. I challenged the students with, "I have an assignment for you. Please read it carefully and do exactly what the directions say. I have written it in such a way that everything should be absolutely clear to you. After the assignment is handed in, we'll see if there was any confusion about the directions." Writing that assignment with absolute clarity was challenging for me. Those students who want a verbal explanation instead of reading for clarity were also challenged. We had quite a revealing discussion afterward about the meanings of *implicit* and *explicit*.

GOAL SETTING—Adapt to any age group. I have used this for 2nd through 12th grade with appropriate changes.

Hand out to each student a sheet of canary yellow unlined paper and a red fine point marker. According to expert salespeople, the mind focuses better with red on yellow.

But do what works best for you.

Instructions to students:

1. *Place the paper horizontally. At the top of the page, write the title My Goals.*

2. *Using a ruler or straightedge, draw a line down the middle vertically and one across the middle horizontally. At the top of each section, label that section with an individual goal that is personal and important to you.* [Write some suggested categories on the board to give them ideas, but make sure they feel free to choose their own: Family, Friends, School, Spirituality, Income, Grades, etc. You may want to ask the class for suggestions.] *In case some of you have a money goal, be specific. An amount of money is not a good goal; what you want to accomplish with the money is the goal. Make this personal to you—not what your parents want or what your teachers want, but what you want. Goals should be attainable. I want to turn into a butterfly might not be realistic. I want to be a free spirit might be.*

3. *Under each goal, write down three Objectives and three Strategies* (You might use less for elementary classes.)

Example for middle/junior high and high school:

Goal: Be a more compassionate friend.
- *I will be a better listener when my friends need me.*
- *When my friend calls me, I will focus on what they are saying.*
- *I will ask questions to help them explain their problem.*
- *I will nurture my friendships.*
- *I will remember my friends' birthdays.*
- *I will spend time with them.*
- *I will always stick up for my friends.*
- *If other kids gossip about my friends, I will be on the right side.*
- *I will only say kind things to others about my friends.*

[You get the idea; make the example grade-appropriate.]

Four goals at a time may be enough to focus on. When you see yourself getting close to accomplishing one or more goals, set new ones. Keep up the momentum.

If a strategy isn't working, or you decide a goal you've selected is not worthwhile, change it. This should be a work in progress. Nothing is set in concrete, but don't change it because of laziness or lack of motivation.

I recommend that you go over your goals every day. Right before you go to sleep at night is an excellent time to program your "superconscious."

NOTE—Students may want to create their Goal Sheets on the computer with personalized graphic designs. Just make sure they are focusing on the goals more than merely coming up with something that looks fancy and takes too much time. Remind them this is a work in progress and should be updated often.

A few times a week, give students time to pull out their goal sheets and silently remind themselves of their targets and to make any necessary changes.

Let students know they are free to share their successes with the class.

GRADING PAPERS, 6TH-12TH—No one outside of teaching (except their families) understands the inordinate amount of time needed for grading papers. Here are some time-saving tips I've learned:

- One of the best ways to truly connect with students is to take time one-on-one to discuss their work. Meet with a few students each week and rotate so that everyone has the opportunity to have your attention.

- Stop and think about how you are going to follow up before you give an assignment. Sixth graders, and sometimes 4th & 5th, can be taught to do peer grading. Use that as much as possible.

See sections on *Writer Responder* and *Writing/Peer Editing Circles* for grades 6th-12th. With proper instruction, students can become quite proficient at grading, editing, and helping their peers.

- **Attn: English teachers**—If you are used to making student papers bleed, may I suggest you get over it. Use a different color pen; my color is purple. Try green, a welcoming, calm color. Most students only look at their grade. A small percentage of conscientious students will take time to learn from your editing their papers. Use *Writer-Responder* or editing circles as much as possible. Or if you insist on putting your pen to their papers, focus on one or two items: one in content, e.g., plot, characterization, etc. and one in mechanics, e.g., commas, incomplete sentences, etc. Rotate focus with each assignment.

- Have an IN BOX for each subject (elementary) or for each class (secondary) for turning in work, and an OUT BOX for returning work. That way you don't take precious instruction time for collecting and returning papers. Students will quickly learn to turn in papers as soon as they enter, and there are always students willing to pass out papers. All of this can be done while you are taking attendance.

- For secondary, at the beginning of each class, have a five-to-ten-minute meaningful activity. I dislike the term *sponge activity*—it sounds meaningless. The Internet has an abundance of worthwhile short exercises that are pertinent to your forthcoming lesson. For secondary, I suggest an *in-context/relevant vocabulary exercise*. These are not graded, but students know they will be held accountable weekly or whenever you decide to do a check, perhaps as part of a curriculum unit test.

- After years of arguing with students who "said" they turned in their paper but you know they didn't, or else tried to turn it in after a deadline, I developed a system that worked 99% of the time. During lunch or as soon as you have a break (during passing- time unless you have hall duty), use a date stamp with your initials and stamp each page in the bottom corner. You can have these made at an office supply store or online for little cost. It will save you an amazing amount of time and angst. You will need to keep your stamp in a safe place.

- Have a consistent system for late work, e.g., excused absences get full credit with a mutual understanding of a new deadline. Unexcused absences do not get credit. Be sure to check your school policy on this before you announce your policy to the students and parents.

- I know the next one may sound unreasonable, but especially for upper grades, this is important. Strive to have a turnaround time of no more than 48 hours, 72 hrs. max, for returning papers.

- Have an organized system that works for YOU so that you *never ever lose student papers.* On the odd chance that you do happen to lose a paper, fess up and work it out with that student in private. Be fair, be honest.

- Now, the big one—Do not neglect yourself, your spouse, or your family by putting teaching first. I love teaching; I love creating new lesson plans; I love thinking up meaningful projects. I told myself I could get by on very little sleep; I love doing it all, and I thought I could do it all. That takes a mighty toll on you and your loved ones. Be wise in how you plan, the hours you spend, and take care of your health.

All you can do is all you can do, and all you can do is enough!
Art Williams

HOMEWORK—Think it through for the sake of the students as well as your own. Let's talk lower grade first. **K-2:** Homework...really? They need to go outside and play when they get home. *Just don't do it. If you have good classroom management skills,* all students should be able to finish work during school time. Encourage fun reading for 15-20 minutes per day at home. That's it! **3-6:** Minimal homework; work on math flash cards and reading; extra time for special projects. Otherwise, *if you have good classroom management skills,* students should be able to finish regular coursework in school. **7-9:** Some homework is necessary. *If you have good classroom management skills,* no more than two hours tops total for all classes should be assigned. **10-12:** Here's where you need to be reasonable. Assigning a big project or test? Talk to the students about their other class work and let them help you decide a date that works for all. They will appreciate your concern and fairness.

If they have jobs, extracurricular activities, girlfriends, that's a choice they are making; *not your problem.* However, if an immediate family member is ill or extenuating circumstance arise, work out something privately and confidentially with that student.

INTERCOM INTERRUPTIONS—You should have infrequent intercom or telephone interruptions. If they become excessive, jot down dates, times, and reasons for the call. After a few days of this, make an appointment to discuss the situation with your administrator. If that doesn't solve the problem, talk to your colleagues and garner support. Then take it to a faculty meeting for discussion.

J-CURVE—Teach on the J-Curve. Forget the infamous Bell Curve that predicts a middle ground with failures on one side and successes on the other. This promotes mediocrity. Think of a "J" where students begin and continue to rise. *All students can succeed.* See *Glasser Quality Schools.*

JOY WAND—A 2nd grader brought me a wand made out of pipe cleaners and sparkly ribbon. She said, "You can use this to tap anyone on the head who is not having joy. And if you are grouchy, you can tap it on your own head so you can have joy, too." It worked wonders to boost moods in the classroom and for me, too. I still have the wand. What a creative, thoughtful little girl.

LIBRARY—Make friends with your school librarian and your local public librarian(s). I give extra credit to students who have a public library card and do what I can to accommodate those students who live where they have to pay a fee or need transportation to get there. Parent volunteers are usually willing to help out. I have worked with exceptional librarians—those who are willing to work with your schedule, assist with projects, including research papers, and even do story time. I have also worked with grumpy librarians who don't want their library to get out of order and even one who asked me not to come back because I wore her out with all of my projects. For the most part, they want to be of service. Writing thank-you cards from your students is always appreciated.

The best teachers are those who show you where to look, but don't tell you what to see. Alexandra K. Trenfor

MATH AUCTION—At the end of every semester, 3rd thru 5th grades, I held a math auction. During the semester, students were awarded play money for various benchmarks. At my request, parents sent in puzzles, books, games, and gently used fun items. On the day of the auction, students learned to carefully plan what they wanted, calculate how much money they had, decide how badly they wanted an item, and make a decision to purchase or not. Math Auction Day (the last two hours of the school day)—was always very exciting. Nothing was ever left unsold. The motivating factor was the recognition they got when they reached a known benchmark, one that the teacher has set and communicated clearly to the class.

MISTAKES MADE BY YOU—Be a good role model and admit it. Then apologize. No excuses. No rationalizing.

MYSTERY BOX [See *Connect with Students on the First Day.*] Prizes: If more than one student gets a correct answer, draw for prizes. Ideas: Useful things like pens/pencils/mechanical pencil lead (always popular), holiday items, weird colors of fingernail polish, snacks—be creative. Let the winner choose from the box of goodies. In elementary grades, ask parents to contribute white elephants, books, puzzles, etc. I love the dollar stores.

Example Questions:
- What happened on this day? Give date. [See www.onthisday.com]
- Choose a category or activity; don't give the website to students.

▢   Find out the birthday of the principal, custodian, etc.
     Question:

▢   Why is _____ an important date?

▢   Who created the happy face icon and what did they get paid
     for it?

NEW STUDENTS—As a student, I changed schools 26 times K-12. I know what I'm talking about. If you have ever changed schools, you may remember how it feels to be the newbie. All eyes are on you, and you feel their questions: *Who are you? Will I like you? Will you like me? Where are you from? Why are you wearing that? What a geek! Look at those dorky shoes.* Take time to help the new student get acclimated. [See *Worm Game.*] Ask for volunteers or assign a student to be a mentor to show the newbie the ropes by explaining classroom routines and assignments. Make sure the new student knows where the bathrooms and cafeteria are and has someone to eat lunch with. I kept a diary my 8th grade year and still have it. For six weeks, I wrote one sentence each day: *I ate by myself again today.* Okay, I was shy, but by 8th grade, I had given up making friends; this particular bunch of students was not overly friendly; and none of my teachers made an effort to see that I was fitting in. Finally, a sweet loner and I connected, and we became best buds. Until then, I was a silent misfit. I made up my mind as a teacher that none of my new students would go through that. If you're one of the fortunate ones to have lived in one or two towns your entire life, please have a heart and look out for the newbies.

PARENT CONFERENCES—Here's a suggestion. A couple of days before parent conferences, give each student a 5 x 7 index card. Ask them to write their name, their parent/guardian names, and a place for their preferred contact number. Then ask students to tell their parents to write down on the card if they have a particular talent they'd like to share with the class at their convenience, or some way they would like to be involved, e.g., chaperoning field trips, making cookies, creating bulletin boards, tutoring, making costumes for a play, etc. Tell the students this is the admission card for their parents at the conference, and that all cards will be put into a big box for a prize drawing for each class. Yes, this is a bribe! Acknowledge it as such if asked. After parent conferences, follow through on the prizes. Then, as soon as possible, call parents to schedule them for the involvement they indicated. Not only will this be valuable information, but it will encourage parents to attend conferences, hopefully with positive attitudes. It may also free up time for you.

PARENT/GUARDIAN CONTACT LOG—See **Appendix** for reproducible example.

PASSES 6-12—The older the students, the fewer bathroom breaks or other passes are needed. Expect students to take responsibility for personal needs between classes. See suggestion for using Calendar Planners in *Connect with Students on the First Day.*

PHONES—Why is it that when the phone rings, you probably have to walk clear across the room to answer it? Do yourself a favor by getting the extra wire and running it around the room or across the ceiling (above the ceiling tiles?) so that you can have the phone near your desk. The extra wire is not expensive, and the decreased stress for you is well worth a few bucks. While we're on the subject, if you have an unruly student, get the daytime phone number and permission from the parent to call them at work or home. Students get a first warning. After that, right at that moment, go to the phone and call the parent. "Hello, Susie isn't behaving in class. Please talk to her." Hand Susie the phone and let the parent take care of it. While Susie is on the phone, give her privacy while you engage the class. No, you didn't humiliate the student; the student chose that. Once is usually enough to let all students know they don't want that to happen to them. This works best when you have the okay from parents to call. **Note:** School districts vary regarding whether or not teachers may use cell phones in the classroom. Consult your administrator or handbook.

RECESS K-5—Do not ever keep students from recess for missing work or for discipline. Elementary age students need to run and play. Use other methods to accomplish helping the student be successful.

RESEARCH—When a student shares seemingly new information, ask them to document where they got it. Internet? What's the source and how do you know it's true? Teach them to seek out primary resources. Also, be ready when you give them information to provide your resources. Encourage them to challenge you.

Responsive Journaling for Reading Fiction or Non-Fiction

Instruction for students:
- Fill a loose-leaf notebook with several pieces of lined paper as follows; add pages as necessary.
- Draw a line vertically down the page. Label the left side *Quotation* and the right side *Response*.

NOTE: The word *quote* is a verb, e.g., Many people *quote* Shakespeare. The word *quotation* is a noun, e.g., This is a *quotation* from Shakespeare. Asides, or incidental learning, are sometimes what students remember best from a teaching session. Always take advantage of those "incidentally, that reminds me" moments. If you get carried away, it's called a bird-walk. Kids are experts at "taking the teacher for a walk." Ya gotta love it! And now, back to responsive journaling...

- On the left side, the student chooses a passage from the reading and writes a quotation, using proper formatting, i.e., quotation marks, proper use of ellipses if the quotation is very long, and page number(s) where the quotation was found.

- On the right side, the student writes a question or response, from their own original thinking, in response to the quotation. Student signs name or initials, owning that response.

- Journal may be entirely personal, even marking a passage "confidential" which everyone agrees to honor. *Integrity—my favorite word.*

- Journal may be shared by other students reading the same book or piece of writing, and each takes a turn at writing quotations/responses, even responding to each other's responses. This can be very motivating for reluctant readers or writers and gratifying for those who love it.

- Encourage students to keep their journals forever. Their grandchildren will want to read them.

ROLE MODELING—Be careful what you say. Your demeanor, body language, and facial expressions speak volumes. Kids are sensitive. Don't call names, even in humor, e.g., *Settle down, you knuckleheads.*

Children need more models than critics.
Joubert

SCIENCE FAIR IDEA—This can be held at your school. However, I once held it at the nearby mall—right down the middle of the entire mall. Yes, it was a LOT of work but extremely gratifying. Parents and students talked about it for months. Students chose a theme, e.g., Save the Dolphins, How Your Heart Works, What Makes a Rainbow, Nutrition, etc.—something each was interested in and their choice (with approval by me, of course.) I gave them the requirements; we worked on it during science class every day for six weeks, including practicing presentations and answering questions. Students were required to have visuals; all had to be neat, clearly stated, and error-free.

Students dressed up. Parents were invited; the entire school took a field trip to attend; the community was invited via the newspaper and posters on community bulletin boards. I have to confess that my principal was less than supportive: *Why would you want to go to all that trouble? We don't have a budget for that. How will we handle transportation?* I convinced him with a little speech about what great PR it would be for him and the school. And, yes, he took full credit at the school board meeting. That was fine. The students and parents were proud of their work, and we were all totally gratified with the outcome.

NOTE: I absolutely forbid expensive fancy presentation boards with brass brackets put together by a well-meaning parent. Students need to do all of their own presentation set-ups.

SKIT IDEA—At the end of the first quarter, I was told it was my turn to do a skit for the school assembly. What to do? Of course, a rap. So, I wrote one that incorporated our school spirit motto. I'm afraid I got a bit carried away; it was long. Would the students want to do it? What a stupid question on my part. They memorized it within a few days, practiced with unabashed enthusiasm, and for the assembly decided to wear school colors, sunglasses, and baseball hats forward, backward, or sideways. How cool! When I asked for a student to lead out, shy awkward Kendall raised his hand. To my surprise, and a slap on my hand for thinking otherwise, Kendall rose to the occasion like an experienced choir director. The class was the hit of the year. Teachers K-5 wanted copies to teach their students, and the entire student body performed it at the last assembly of the year. After the assembly, I spoke with Kendall's mother, praising him to the hilt.

"Oh, yes," she said, "he's the drummer in our church band and leads out all the time." Shame on me for doubting his ability just because he was a quiet child. Lesson learned!

Here's the RAP:

SOAR with Spirit

Come along with us now

Learn this song, sing it proud:

We're the Cottonwood Kids

We're the Eagles, watch us SOAR

We're the Cottonwood Kids

We're the Eagles, watch us SOAR

S is for Safety, that's the Cottonwood game,

In the halls, on the playground

That's how we get our fame.

Look around, up and down,

We look out for each other

S is for safety, ya gotta care 'bout your brother.

We're the Cottonwood Kids

We're the Eagles, watch us SOAR

We're the Cottonwood Kids

We're the Eagles, watch us SOAR

O is how we Own it,

That's for positives, too.

Whether right or wrong

Wear your red, don't be blue;

Now come right along

Help us sing Cottonwood's song.

We're the Cottonwood Kids

We're the Eagles, watch us SOAR

We're the Cottonwood Kids

We're the Eagles, watch us SOAR

A is for Achievement

That means we do our work,

Go above and beyond

Do it now and don't shirk,

Learning is our duty

Growing dendrites, what a beauty!

R means respect

And that is what we show

For our teachers and the staff--

Please and thank-you is what we know

We take off our hats when we come in the door

We pick up what we drop so we have a clean floor.

Now you've heard what we're about--

We're proud Cottonwood kids,

Let's all give a shout

'Cause we know how to live,

Make our world a better place--

Join us in this joyful space!

Come along with us now

Learn this song, sing it proud.

We're the Cottonwood Kids

We're the Eagles, watch us SOAR

We're the Cottonwood Kids

We're the Eagles, watch us SOAR

The Cottonwood RAP, courtesy of Ms. Walraven's 5th Grade

Feel free to borrow, adapt, change, put to music—whatever works for you.

Note: For teachers' use only.

SIBLINGS—Don't compare siblings…ever! 'Nuf said.

STUDENT FILES—One of the best things you can do for yourself in connecting with students is to learn as much about each one as quickly as you can. Take time before or after school, during lunch, whenever you can grab a few minutes. Go to the office or wherever they keep confidential student records and read the student file. You might be amazed at how it tweaks your connection with that student and prevents possible challenges in the future.

SPELLING—It's a talent, not an academic subject. I can't sing well, but I can spell almost anything. When I'm not sure, I know where to look it up or use spell check. Maybe it's genetic. *What makes a good speller? Knowing when and where to look it up!* Some of the brightest students are not natural spellers. Teach, don't preach! And for goodness sake, don't cover your walls with lists of spelling words. No one looks at them. Teach students to look up words when they need them.

SUICIDE/DRUGS/ILLEGAL BEHAVIOR—This used to be a topic for high school students only, but it seems that our society, especially with social media, has made it something that we might sadly expect at any age. Before you do anything, check with your administration for guidelines. I like having students journal anything they want to write about. After discussing the meaning of *integrity*, something that I value above all else, I assure them that whatever they write will be confidential with one exception. I let them know that if they write about anything that even hints at endangering their own lives or that of someone else, or something illegal, I will first talk to them about it, and we will decide together how to find help for that person or situation. Any student who speaks or writes about any of these, even seemingly as a joke, needs to be taken seriously as a cry for help. Do not ignore that. Handle it confidentially and professionally. *Extreme caution*: If you do not feel you are getting support from your administration or district office, you must report to Child Protective

Services. Be sure to document everything in writing to protect the child and yourself. This paramount duty requires courage.

TESTING—Time Left at End of Session—Train your students to always have with them school work or a book to read if they finish testing ahead of time. They need to practice using time wisely. **Note:** I made an exception for the senior who worked nights; this was nap time for him.

WASTING CLASS TIME—Some students intentionally try to waste class time. This is frustrating for students who have been paying attention and want to get on with the lesson. If the question is relevant to most, take time. If not, tell the student, "Please see me after class (or as soon as we get started on the assignment), and I'll help you individually."

When you tell students to turn to a certain page, write the page number on the board. If a student then asks, "What page?" because they have not been paying attention, ignore their question. That lets them know you expect them to be listening. They'll get the hint.

WRITING—Take a survey of teachers. The general consensus is that students can't write well. Being a good reader doesn't necessarily translate into being a good writer. Again, the cart before the horse. *If you cannot read well, you cannot write well.* You may have good ideas but don't know how to express yourself in writing. Reading correctly and efficiently is essential for understanding and learning all coursework.

Voice—Instruction for students: Work toward a conversational rhythm in your writing. Don't try to emulate, oops, don't try to sound like some published author who wrote in the early 1900s. Find your own voice so that your reader feels like you are talking to them inside their own heads as they read. Your writing *voice* is your personality shining through your words. Sometimes it's difficult to find your *voice*. Relax, and just write like you would say it to a friend in a real conversation. This will lead to your being able to break spelling rules to write in your own dialect. *Ah cain't hep lovin' you.*

We write to taste life twice.
Anais Nin

Writer-Responder Method—This method may be used teacher-to-student or student-to-student during or after class. Teachers in disciplines outside of English who are not comfortable mentoring students, e.g., research papers, sometimes feel inadequate to help students with editing. This way they listen, ask questions, and are more comfortable in making suggestions.

- The student reads their writing to the teacher or another student aloud.
- The listener interrupts with questions, e.g., "What I hear you saying is….Is that what you mean to say?"
- Student corrects their own writing from the suggestions or from hearing him/herself read aloud.
- The listener may take notes but never touches the student's writing.

Correcting student writing—Teacher and students need a good, simple, indexed book of guidelines for grammar, punctuation, capitalization, and spelling. Remember, these guidelines can be learned by anyone, but they are not set in concrete. Many good writers break the rules, but they know them so well that they know when they can break them effectively. Writers need to know *why* they are breaking the rules. Keep the guidebook handy to use as a reference guide. Students need to learn to correct their own errors. For choosing the right handbook for you and your students, see www.hackerhandbooks.com

- In the margin, identify the problem, e.g., *sp* for spelling error, *cap* for capitalization, etc. The student uses the guidebook as a resource to find and correct the problem. Only when the student has expended sufficient energy but cannot "see" what needs to be corrected does the teacher step in to give further guidance but not answers. Be cognizant of the student's frustration level and deal with the frustration but don't give in by correcting the paper for them. Incidentally, the use of the word *them* is now acceptable even if referring to the singular; this takes the place of the awkward him/her. If it bothers you, change the sentence. This question arises regularly.

Example of singular/plural agreement in pronouns as well as possessives:

1. Be aware of the *student's* [singular] frustration level, but don't correct it for *him/her* [singular].
2. Be aware of the *student's* [singular] frustration level, but don't correct it for *them* [acceptable use of plural].
3. Be aware of the students' [plural] frustration levels [plural], but don't correct it for *them* [plural].

▫ Require that the student and teacher both learn and use editing marks. This shorthand will save much time, e.g., three little lines under a letter that needs to be capitalized. The student, not the teacher, makes the editing marks on their own paper. Keep a chart handy in the student notebook and on the wall in the classroom. Numerous editing charts are available online.

▫ Avoid generalizations, e.g., "Never begin a sentence with the words *there* or *it*." This is a good rule that can sometimes be broken very effectively. Writers don't get to use *literary license* to break the rules until they have proved themselves worthy. *It was a dark and stormy night* is still a very effective beginning, but a writer can almost always find a better way to begin a sentence than by using the words *it* or *there*. Flipping the sentence around forces description, allows the writer to be more specific, and the writing becomes more fluid.

Example: *There* was a man standing on the street who was unshaven and old, and he was wearing a tattered sweater. **Better:** The elderly, unshaven man standing on the street looked forlorn in his tattered sweater.

- Young students are often told they cannot begin a sentence with the word *because*. This is erroneous information. Elementary students often do not understand sentence structure and the need for a subject and predicate. As students mature, they may indeed begin sentences with *because*.

Immature usage: I went shopping at the mall. Because I needed a new coat. **Mature:** Because I needed a new coat, I went shopping at the mall.

- Understanding dependent and independent clauses will lead to more sophisticated writing. Use your guidebook and look up *clauses*; understand the difference between a *phrase* and a *clause*. This will also necessitate the proper use of *semicolons*. These words are merely labels that help communicate about language usage. It's not rocket science; learn to use grammar to your advantage.

Editing Sessions

▫ The student agrees to take the time to sit down with you to go over punctuation/grammar/spelling.

▫ Go over rules as you edit with the student; don't merely mark the paper.

▫ The student needs to understand "why" the changes need to be made, e.g., for clarity. Rules don't exist to make a writer's life miserable; they exist to make the writing more understandable. A comma misplaced or omitted has led to incoherence as well as lawsuits.

▫ If there are numerous errors, work on one paragraph at a time or one type of error at a time. Don't let the session feel overwhelming.

▫ Remember: These are just rules. Anyone can learn them. The creative act of writing is a talent; one may improve as with singing lessons, but one may or may not turn out to be a star or have their first novel hit the *NY Times Bestseller List.*

Peer Editing Circles— Works best for middle/high school but younger children can become proficient with training. Teach students to be Writer-Responders [**See Writer-Responder**]. Give them time to pair up and quietly read aloud their writings to each other. Another idea is to have students put their desks in a circle. Announce ahead of time that they must bring their assignment to class or they will sit it out, no reading, no messing around with anything else, i.e., be bored. That kind of peer pressure is effective; they'll want to be included next time.

Students sit in a circle. Each student has a Comment Page for their writing. Pass papers to the left and read silently. Write positive comments/suggestions only on the Comment Page and sign responder name. Students may comment on content and/or mechanics. When finished with one, trade until all papers are read or time is up. If time is limited, have students read only a few paragraphs.

NOTE: If a reluctant student fails a second time to join the circle, pull that student aside to find the cause—Does the student have a place to do homework? Can the student read? Can the student write? See what you can do to motivate the student. Have the student come in outside of class to help them prepare for the next circle activity. They need to experience feeling success so that they want to repeat it.

Enough for now. I have reams of notes, maybe for a second book. If you have special tricks of the trade, please share them with other teachers, especially rookies. Teaching is a hard job. We need to make our classrooms user-friendly for our students and ourselves.

————— ◆ —————

The more open and connected you are to the world around you,
the more creative you become.
Melody Beattie

APPENDIX

Contracts and Logs may be copied for use only by teachers and administrators.

COURTESY CONTRACT

One classroom rule: Courtesy to everyone at all times.

When the tardy bell rings, I am preparing for class; quiet conversation is permitted until the teacher is ready to begin.

During a classroom discussion, I participate in an appropriate way. I ask questions and am willing to venture a guess at answers even if I'm not sure. I keep my mind in gear and use creative thinking.

When an assignment is due, I turn it in on time. If I have an excused absence, *I take the initiative to make arrangements for makeup work.*

My handwritten work is legible, neat, and completed on 3-ring notebook paper (holes intact). I do not use spiral tear-out paper for turn-in assignments because it makes me look like a careless, messy student. Unless otherwise directed, I use a sharp, medium pencil or blue or black ballpoint pen. Keyboarding assignments are completed according to the proper format.

I strive to have a positive attitude toward school, my teachers, and my fellow students and will do all I can to make learning pleasant.

I will do all I can to obtain a QUALITY education at _____
School by

- being cooperative and courteous
- being willing to participate
- being curious, asking questions, and wanting to know more
- keeping an organized notebook and writing down assignments
- learning how to find, review and use available resources
- being persistent and willing to work for quality
- being willing to accept assistance and give assistance
- being a team player by sharing my ideas and listening to others
- accepting responsibility for doing my part in…

the journey toward a quality education.

I have read and understand the stated expectations.

Student Signature _____ Date_____

Parent Signature _____ Date_____

PARENT/GUARDIAN CONTACT LOG

Student Name: _____

Address: _____

Home Phone: _____ Parent(s) Cell: _____

Parent Work Phone: _____, Ext. _____

Okay to call: Yes_____ No_____

Date/Time of Call	Reason for Call	Parent Response

Other parent Call Logs are available online. Keep it in a 3-ring binder close to your phone.

STUDENT CONTRACT FOR SUCCESS

Student:_____Date_____

Teacher:_____Class_____

I agree that I have not been fully cooperative in class.

I have been given ample opportunity to understand, practice, and correct my behavior.

In the future, I agree to abide by classroom rules. I further agree to change my attitude to one of gratitude for this educational opportunity and be a good role model for my classmates.

I understand that failure to live up to my agreement per this contract with teacher(s), parent(s), counselor(s), and administrator(s) will result in further disciplinary action.

I also understand that I am fully capable of becoming a successful student. Signatures of Participants:

Student: _____Date_____
Teacher: _____Date_____
Counselor: _____Date_____
Administrator: _____Date_____

Notes:

ABOUT THE AUTHOR

R. Janet Walraven is not only an accomplished teacher but also an experienced student having attended twenty-six schools across the United States as she grew up traveling with her family. She inherited from her parents a profound desire and appreciation for learning. Teaching was her life; education is her passion. In her next lives, she wants to speak fluent Italian and French, study architecture and astronomy, attempt to understand black holes, become more tuned-in to consciousness and mindfulness, travel the world, and continue to write poetry, short stories, memoir, creative non-fiction, and other fun stuff. For now, her goal is to aid humanitarian endeavors, live a healthy lifestyle, write, write, write, and awaken each morning embracing the JOY of that day.

TESTIMONIALS

FROM A STUDENT'S PERSPECTIVE

Janet Walraven is the most talented and inspiring teacher I've ever known. Thankfully she came into my life at a most agonizing time—dreaded middle school. She had the rare talent of making me feel that she was truly on my side, and she was always excited to discover something new with me. I never felt she was trying to teach me, but rather that we were discovering together. She helped me trust my own mind and to believe in myself. Where other teachers could be impatient with my questioning, she was genuinely delighted! Years later, Janet remains a trusted friend, continuing to be an inspiration and role model for me as I have now become an educator and forever a lifelong learner.

Robbyn Peters Bennet, MA, LMHC, CMHS

[www.StopSpanking.org]

FROM A TEACHER'S PERSPECTIVE

Robbyn sat in my 8th-grade classroom with a hungry look in her eyes. She questioned everything, much of which I did not know how to answer. Her mind challenged every concept, always wanting to know why, how, and always wanting more. She was truly the most inspirational and brightest student I ever taught. Robbyn did not come from a privileged background; quite the opposite. Yet as a single mother, she put herself through school and now follows her passion for educating parents on the extremely negative effects of spanking. I urge you to log onto her website and support her cause.

IN GRATITUDE

Thank you to everyone who encouraged me to share my teaching experience. A special thanks to my sisters, Rita and Ramona—both excellent writers and editors—who assured me that my teaching stories were worth sharing; my parents Bill and Sadina Walraven who believed that education is paramount for succeeding in life; Garrett Bosarge who encouraged and supported me in my teaching experience; Barb and Jim Ruble, lifelong personal and professional role models and advisors; and to Mal Johnson who cheered me on through long hours of writing this manuscript.

A special thanks to my writing partners, Maryann Morie who let me know what did and didn't work in the scenarios, and to Michelle Ann Boelter who edited multiple times, insisted on excellence in writing and organization, shared research on publishing, and held me to the high standard that we have set for ourselves as writers.

Gratitude also to very special K-12 teachers who shaped my learning in significant ways: My kindergarten teacher in Girard KS taught me that school can be a joy; 1st grade, piano teacher, Enid OK; 2nd grade, Ms. Snare, Hereford TX; 4th grade, Ms. Alma Gordon, Paulding OH; 5th grade, Ms. Niederhouse, Hutchinson KS; 6th grade, Ms. Mildred Parker, Albuquerque NM; 10th grade English, Ms. Margaret Griswold, Liberty, MO; 12th grade English, Ms. Doris Ely, Hutchinson KS. Special thanks to Dr. Tim Standal and Dr. Nancy Hanson-Krenig, University of Washington, Seattle, and Linda Quinn, best-ever administrator.

A heartfelt thank-you to all of my colleagues and students who taught me more about teaching and about life than I could have learned anywhere else.

I am also over-the-top grateful to Dr. Dee Tadlock, creator of **Read Right**® methodology. Her program has positively impacted the lives of tens of thousands of children and adults. Using **Read Right** in my teaching has been a highlight of my career and continues to be a personal passion.

For a while, after retiring from teaching, I mentored teachers. That was the main reason I felt compelled to write this book. If this book can help even one teacher succeed with quality and pleasure-centered learning, it will have been worth the effort. Thank you, Toakase Vunileva, for trusting me with a most gratifying challenge in mentoring.

A shout-out also to author/teacher Sarah Baker for her encouragement and expertise in publishing and editing. Also, to Larry and Charmaine Estes for producing the video for my mentoring website.

Writing is a joy; rewriting and editing for quality is a worthwhile task. If you are reading this right now, please accept my gratitude. I hope it in some way enhances your world.

———— ♦ ————

Our schools must preserve and nurture the yearning for
learning that we are born with. Joy in learning comes not so
much from what is learned, but from learning.
W. Edwards Deming

REQUEST FOR REVIEWS

Thank you for your interest in **CONNECT FOR CLASSROOM SUCCESS**.

If you found this information interesting, helpful, or have someone in mind who could benefit from it, I would very much appreciate a review on Amazon.

R. Janet Walraven

Made in the USA
San Bernardino, CA
11 August 2020

76221090R00115